MW00977950

THE
DOXA
METHOD

TRANSPORT YOUR FEARS
INTO SUCCESS!

ANA WEBER

Edited by Shel Horowitz of Going Beyond Sustainability

Cover design by Andrea McNeeley – 320: designs

BALBOA.
PRESS
A DIVISION OF HAY HOUSE

Balboa Press books may be ordered through booksellers or by contacting:

Balboa Press
A Division of Hay House
1663 Liberty Drive
Bloomington, IN 47403
www.balboapress.com
1 (877) 407-4847

Because of the dynamic nature of the Internet, any web addresses or links contained in this book may have changed since publication and may no longer be valid. The views expressed in this work are solely those of the author and do not necessarily reflect the views of the publisher, and the publisher hereby disclaims any responsibility for them.

The author of this book does not dispense medical advice or prescribe the use of any technique as a form of treatment for physical, emotional, or medical problems without the advice of a physician, either directly or indirectly. The intent of the author is only to offer information of a general nature to help you in your quest for emotional and spiritual well-being. In the event you use any of the information in this book for yourself, which is your constitutional right, the author and the publisher assume no responsibility for your actions.

Any people depicted in stock imagery provided by Thinkstock are models, and such images are being used for illustrative purposes only. Certain stock imagery © Thinkstock.

Print information available on the last page.

ISBN: 978-1-5043-8754-5 (sc)
ISBN: 978-1-5043-8753-8 (hc)
ISBN: 978-1-5043-8752-1 (e)

Library of Congress Control Number: 2017914079

Balboa Press rev. date: 03/05/2018

Contents

Section 1
Life before The DOXA METHOD

Section 2
THE DOXA METHOD

Section 3
THE DOXA METHOD life
with the DOXA METHOD

DEDICATION

I dedicate this book to all the people in the world who seek personal liberty and happiness.

Ana Weber

ACKNOWLEDGEMENTS

Thank you to my husband, Mario for his continued support, awesome devotion and tremendous patience.

It's been a tough year for you and regardless to unexpected challenges you expressed your genuine efforts and love.

I AM delighted to acknowledge and express my love and my appreciation to my son Sean, and my two grandchildren, Logan and Mia.

You are my greatest gift and I am looking forward to many happy and joyful years spent with you traveling the world.

Very special thanks to Shel Horowitz. I am so blessed to work with him and to have him as a dear brilliant friend. Thank you so

I would like to thank David Thalberg for believing in me, for his amazing guidance, and for his continued support and efforts.

Many thanks to Shelley Hunt, Linda Hollander and Jackie Lapin.

Ana Weber

THE DOXA METHOD
- 3 SECTIONS

SECTION 1
Life before The
DOXA METHOD

Chapter 1
From Darkness to Light

"Why are you crying?" Mom gave me a serious look. "You know it's all going to work out." I took out my handkerchief, dried my eyes, and continued to cross Tel Aviv's broad, congested Allenby Street.

I was 10 going on 11, a child in years but shouldering the burdens of an adult. Confronting the challenges of our existence—creating a new life in a new country, going back to school, and finding food for our table—my anxiety was understandable.

We were destitute and friendless, enveloped in uncertainty.

Back then, I didn't realize how much of an optimist my mom was. Her behavior and her attitude allowed her faith, her trust and her courage to shine through. Nothing would ever break her spirit! Mom survived the Holocaust—the worst of all life events. Nothing could compare to that trauma. She lost family members, not to mention an aristocratic life in a secure, beautifully decorated, large home with servants.

She was the 16th child of two amazing parents. My grandfather was a scholar and a leader in Hungary's and Czechoslovakia's grape cultivation business. He was a leader ahead of his time. An educated man with deep knowledge in many areas, he was inspired by his vision of helping to create a mature wine industry in the country. Also educated and elegant, my grandmother, born into the elite Esterhazy Eisenstaedt family, lectured weekly to women's groups.

Mom grew up with calmness, beauty, and tremendous love. But her perfect life had slammed shut abruptly and painfully.

Yet, that awesome foundation kept her sane at the worst of times. After the war, every obstacle and challenge was nothing to her. "The worst is over," she would say. She could handle any situation. Regardless of its difficulty, she overcame it with flying colors and moved on. Mom loved life and believed that even a bare life is more than no life at all.

Though I learned so much from her, my childhood was very different from hers. The same obstacles that made me fearful were just chances to show her high spirit, her enthusiasm for life, and her active mind.

Just a few hours before, we'd arrived at Tel Aviv's airport from Cluj, Romania. It was our very first flight. Mom held my hand and prayed the entire time. She tried not to show her fear—but I could sense it in her shaking, cold hands.

Just the two of us, flying to a whole new life. My parents had divorced when I was 5. I felt the loneliness more than ever.

I will never forget Dad's face when we hugged and said good bye to each other. At the time, I had long brown hair braded in the back and a thin face with brown eyes and pale skin. "Would you mind if I kept your braid with me as a souvenir of your pretty face?" Dad asked. "After all, you are moving to a warm place, it might be easier and less warm to keep short hair." Mom glanced at me. Without a word, she walked over to the kitchen area, took out the large scissors from the drawer, and proceeded to cut my hair.

I said nothing. The reflection in our illuminated custom-made snake-shaped gold-plated mirror matched my feeling of nakedness.

I can still recall the feeling. It was a new emotion: a sense of letting go and of welcoming the opportunity, to newness. Yet, at the same time, I was full of doubts. But I listened to my innocent inner voice and asked no questions.

The next day we were on a train to Hungary and off to Austria. After seven days in Austria, we boarded the plane in Vienna, the city covered with clear snow, cold seeping through our bodies. Since the temperature was 10 below zero, we wore scarves, boots, warm clothes, and tight wool hats with matching gloves. The flight was long but steady.

We'd arrived at Tel Aviv early in the morning on January 13th, 1960, stepped off the plane, and touched the Promised Land. A place filled with dreams and possibilities! We both kissed the ground, with a sense of liberty. We did it! This was it! We'd embarked on a new unfamiliar life. Who knew what was in store?

We were greeted with 80-degree weather and a *chamsin*, (hot wind) blowing from the west. Unprepared for such hospitality, we peeled off our layers and we still felt overheated, desperate for a bath and a cold drink somewhere.

Dad believed that relocating to a new country following Mom's dream would be a great change and would lead to an easier life for me.

Little he knew that the first few months would be unbearable.

From the immigration department, Mom received $100, along with keys to a small flat out in Yavne, some canned olives, marmalade, matzo, and a block of old cheese. We were supposed to be thrilled and excited about the small *shikun* (1 bedroom flat) we got free and clear of obligations)—but the flat was out in an open land, miles away from school, civilization, grocery stores, or public transportation. All we could see were unpaved roads, lots of sand, and the eerie feeling of walking through a large desert.

A few hours later, Mom and I returned the keys, closed the door to the flat, and took the bus to Tel Aviv in search of Mom's elder sister. But she and her husband had moved to a new place without leaving a forwarding address. So here we were, alone, without a decent home, a bath and proper food to eat. And that's why crossing Allenby Street was one of the most emotional and difficult things I'd ever done. Carrying a small suitcase each, Mom and I were heading to the Vittman Ice Cream parlor.

Holding tightly to the money and with shaking hands, Mom handed me a few coins.

"Go ahead," she said. "Ask for a chocolate milkshake for each of us. It will sweeten our spirit and it might even give us some ideas to where shall we go next."

Not speaking the local language, we felt and looked like foreigners, our vulnerability and unfamiliarity streaming clearly thorough our entire being. I spoke Hungarian, Romanian, French and Russian—but not a word of Hebrew. Mom had an advantage; she also spoke Yiddish and German.

When I handed the coins to the man behind the counter he smiled. I pointed to the milkshake photo and showed 2 fingers up. He understood and within minutes we had two delicious shakes. We walked over to the table and sat down.

I didn't remember a day when I'd felt so tired as that very moment. Mom looked drained and exhausted. We slowly sipped in silence until we began to regain some energy—and converse about the meager but sufficient life we'd left behind in Romania: Mother's cigarette, newspaper, and magazine kiosk and my athletic achievements running track. We talked about our favorite operas, movies, and classical ballet. Mom did not have a profession; she'd been raised with the idea that women need to be taken care of by their husbands and run a home. But after my parents divorced, Mom had to get a job and support the two of us. It was Communism, and no choices were presented.

So here we were, enjoying that milkshake and cooling off our minds and bodies.

We had no plans, direction, or destination and we were not in a hurry to get anywhere. The bottomless freedom we felt was an illusion,   covering our fear and desperation. The heaviness that filled the air was my first recollection of anxiety. Only years later I understood what it meant, along with my racing heartbeat.

We were almost done with our chocolate milkshakes when a handsome young man strode over to our table. He looked like a GQ model: polished black shoes, a fine tailored grey suit, a red tie and a white striking shirt.

"How are you? Where you are going and what languages do you speak?" he asked in Yiddish. I didn't understand the questions. Mom didn't answer at first and her look wasn't friendly.

A few seconds later, Mom answered politely.

Her response brought a huge smile to his face. "I can see you are in a bad place and with no home to go to, two little suitcases on the floor by your side. I can change all that for you."

Mom looked worried.

He continued. "I can take care of your daughter and

give her a place and a good life out of this country. You will be paid a nice sum of money and be free of worrying about her. I know she is merely a child but she has great potential. She looks mature and pretty, with a young woman's shape already. Is she 13?

To put it bluntly, he was really saying, "Sell your girl to me—and life will become easier for you. You will unite someday but not for a few years. I will keep in touch with you."

A stormy silence broke the air and Mom began to cry like I'd never seen before. Fixing him in a withering, piercing gaze, she raised her hands and shouted, "Get away from us! You are from the darkness of life. She is all I have. How dare you come to us? There is no money in the world to replace her existence. I lost most of my family members a few years back. Get out!" And then her anger became even more intense, her screams even louder. "You are not a human being, only dressed up as one. Leave now!"

The man walked away—and out of our lives forever. In the silence, I listened to our hearts ticking.

Once the drama had ended, a young man in uniform at the next table walked over with a cold glass of water for Mom. She calmed down and began to translate the event for me. As I listened incredulously, I understood that a priceless human bond is too precious to trade.

While all the other witnesses sat frozen in their seats (in shock, perhaps), the young man asked the ice cream parlor owner to bring over a few of his home baked cookies. Nothing had ever tasted better. These sweets would replace the sour taste of that awful interchange.

The sun was ready to take a nap and we had no place to put our heads down. But the young man worked another miracle for us; he offered to let us stay in his apartment for a few nights. "Things will work out," he said. But Mom shook her head. "I will go over to one of my work friends," he insisted. "He has a larger apartment—a perfect place for both of us." The store owner confirmed that he'd known the man for several years and staying with him would be safe. He taught high school Hebrew and history. Man, did I need his help!

We walked over to his apartment, carrying our few belongings and our hope for a brighter tomorrow.

His apartment was on the third floor. As he opened the door for us, I threw myself on the little bed, filled with gratitude. "Thank you," I said in Hungarian and he smiled. He showed us the small kitchen area with a small stove, a tiny refrigerator. Next to it was a small bathroom with a shower, sink and toilet, barely big enough to get through.

He turned his small radio on. A Mozart concerto was playing gently. At last, I felt at home.

The young man's name was Yechiel, meaning God lives. Mom and I took showers, changed our clothes, and fell asleep for the night. We'd marched from darkness to light in just a couple of hours. Today, more than 5 decades later, I still remember that evening and the taste I felt. For the first time in my life, I was exposed to the two extremes of good and evil, both standing and claiming their power. How close they were—and how profound!

But we had made our choice. God had shown us the path to faith and so much more.

The lessons of that first evening shaped my life; they rumbled my soul and my spirit—and still help me navigate my lifetime journey through a wheel colored with faith, painted with trust and designed with the wisdom to share.

After a big morning feast, Yechiel asked, "what would you like to do today? I have the day off so I can help you with anything you need. On Wednesday's I usually take a long walk, spend time with my friends and shop for groceries."

Mom answered, clearly and firmly. "Well, it would be great to find my sister. How about going to the local police station to ask?"

"Great idea. Let's do it." A few minutes later, as we were descending the stairs, an elderly woman flung open the door of her ground-floor apartment. stepped out to confront Yechiel. "Who are these young ladies?" she asked with an unfriendly smile. "You know better. When you rented the apartment, you signed the lease specifying 1 person and no nighttime visitors."

"Yes, I invited these ladies to stay. They are new, fresh

immigrants in the country and had nowhee to go so I offered to let them stay until they find their relatives," Yechiel replied.

There was an unpleasant silence, until she turned directly to us and said, "I could use some help in my apartment. Do you know how to cook European dishes?" she asked Mom. "And you, little girl, do you know how to dust furniture and wash the tile floors? By the way, my name is Sybil."

"I cook Hungarian and Romanian food," Mom replied. "I am passionate about cooking but I never cooked for anyone else or for money or for a roof over our heads." Shy, introvert girl that I was, I remained silent.

Sybil told Mom, "I will let you stay here for a month. You cook for me and the girl will help me clean the two-bedroom apartment, the kitchen, the bathroom, and the balcony. You will also have one meal a day, but the rest you will have to provide for yourself. In a nutshell cooking 5 hours a week and cleaning 3 -5 hours a week will be fine with me."

Temporary as it was, the timing was perfect. We

agreed to the terms. "We will start tomorrow," Mom said. We waved good-bye. As we headed out to the street, Mom apologized softly. "I never thought I would ever do this and you are too young for manual labor, but within a month, many things will come our way. It's okay, we cannot afford to say no. Yechiel nodded and I smiled. Mom cooked for Sybil and I learned to clean the apartment. The manual labor was new to me but I didn't mind. I felt so much older and accomplished.

At the police station, an officer tracked down my aunt and uncle's address within 30 minutes. "They live in Givatayim," the police officer commented. "It's Hamifne 6, a 20 minutes bus ride, approximately." We were elated.

"What does it mean, Hamifne?" Mom asked Yechiel.

"Interestingly enough, it means "turning," he answered. We all smiled.

"It's certainly a turning point for us," Mom said, "you'll see, Ana. It will all be great. I feel it. Signs everywhere to guide us on our journey—who would have thought?"

Not wanting to intrude on our reunion, Yechiel did not come up with us.

25 minutes later, my Aunt Gizy opened her apartment door, gazing at Mom and me with love and amazement. "Oh my God, you're here! What a surprise!"

She introduced us to her husband, who was recuperating from heart surgery and wasn't at his best. He barely spoke. My aunt's apartment was cozy and very well furnished. She had a fairly large kitchen, a small bedroom, a living room a tiny bedroom with a bathroom adjoining, and a lovely balcony overlooking the street.

Gizy prepared us sandwiches and bananas. It was my very first time eating a banana—and it was instant love. After eating two bananas I had no desire for the sandwich. "This is so delicious," I announced, "I will live on bananas from now on—a fruit of joy, and so protected." Everyone smiled.

My aunt made some fresh orange juice and took us outside to the balcony for a serious conversation: "What are you going to do," she asked Mom. Your daughter needs to go to school and you have no profession. What are your plans? To be frank, I cannot have you stay here. Our place is for two people and my husband has no desire to add more tenants. He needs to heal." We got the message, loud and clear.

Gizy suggested we contact my cousin Yona, who lived near Tel Aviv. "He has a big home, with a yard, two boys close to your daughter's age, and a lovely wife. Here is the address. I know he will take you both in until you get on your feet." Yona translates as dove—how cool is that?

And so he did. Keeping our promise to Sybil, Mom and I moved to his home after a month.

We moved in on February 15, 1960. It was a light winter and the place felt magical. Not only were we welcomed, we even had our own bedroom with a large window overlooking the backyard. I started learned a bit of Hebrew from my second cousins and began to feel less of a stranger.

The city we moved to was Tzahala, which meant "the cough." Looking back, I understand today that my cousin's place gave us our first opportunity to cough up the old and bring in new possibilities along the way.

Two weeks later, Yona invited us to sit at the table in the backyard. His wife Rachel served us grapefruit juice, her homemade cheesecake, and some tangerines. Mom and I were beginning to get used to the various tropical foods, the different weather, and all the other changes.

Yona spoke to Mom in Hungarian. "So here we go. I believe that vacation time is over. Your daughter Ana needs to go to school, learn the language here, and get some independence."

Mom asked; "What do you mean? What are your intentions? I know we can't stay here forever."

"Well, I have contacts with the administrative leaders running Kfar Batya, a *moshav* [commune] for children Ana's age and a bit older. The kids are immigrants, children of poor parents, children of single parents, and orphans. Ana will go to school half the day. She will work 4 hours a day and sleep in a dorm with 3 other girls, with a detached bathroom shared with other dorms. It's a religious place, where kids are taught the Bible, prayer and spirituality.

Turning to me, he continued, "I believe it's going to be phenomenal for you, Ana.

"And you my dear aunt, you need to maintain yourself and find some work and become less codependent on us."

Mom dropped her fork with a look of despair: "When will this all take place, how far is Kfar Batya from Tel Aviv, and where could I possibly find good work and a place to live?"

Feeling her pain but standing strong in his convictions, Yona replied, "Let's get Ana situated next week. Hopefully, within a few weeks, you will find something to do. I believe you can help out with children, or get into catering or work at a home for the aging."

The following week, my cousin Yona drove us to Kfar Batya.

It was a farm way out in the country. As a lifelong city dweller, I could not imagine for a minute living there or adjusting to the surroundings. But Yona assured me that eventually I'd love it. I'd learn so much about survival, independence, studies, work, and prayer.

After I got settled, the manager showed us around. For the first time in my life, I saw chickens, turkeys, geese, and ducks running around. The moshav had large citrus trees, banana trees, large vegetable gardens. The campus also included a big dining room, dorms in small buildings, uncut grass, work buildings for ironing, washing, and sewing—and a place of prayer with large stained windows and a wide big door.

To top off the strangeness, we had to wear uniforms and matching shoes. Our belongings were locked up in our personal stations as the new identity took hold. Not to mention, I had to learn a totally foreign and deeply frustrating language with a new alphabet with simple artistic letters that read from right to left. 'Will I ever learn this language?' I would ask myself. Why is it so different from all the European languages I'd mastered? What's really special about these letters?

Only much later in life, when I studied the Talmud and the Kabbalah, did I realize how powerful those letters are, and how much wisdom is in a system that gives every letter and every word a numerical value.

Neither Mom nor I cried when she left me there—but our hearts were filled with tears and unspoken words.

We had to let go and move on. No complaining. After choosing a life in Israel, we had to roll with punches.

A short, serious woman walked me around the entire complex. Each compact dormitory room housed four girls, and we each had a small wooden cabinet.

But when I saw the shower and bathroom facilities, I froze. 20 girls shared each floor's big bathroom with a shower, bathtub, and toilet right next to the shower.

Back in Romania, we'd shared our bathroom with just two other families. Mom used to wash our faces, hair, and bodies with rainwater. "It's gentle to the skin," she'd say— and I loved it. she would. Mom saved the rain water in big metal tubs, heating it for our weekly baths so we could enjoy this luxury at least three to five months of the year.

Cleary, this ritual would be impossible at the moshav. And sharing with 19 other girls seemed overwhelming.

"Here is the soap," the woman barked. "It's a big bar and it's supposed to last for a month."

The huge brown bar was rough. It looked heavy and scratchy. If I dropped the soap, I could break my foot! Even though we'd shared a bathroom in Romania, each family owned our own soaps. It felt more inviting and less intimidating.

"You can take a 3 minute shower and no more, including your hair." Fortunately, my hair was short and manageable at the time. "We're dividing you into three groups. Seven girls will take their shower in the early morning, the next seven girls will take their showers after work before going to school, and the remaining six girls will take their shower at night before going to bed. The list will be placed on the bathroom door and you will have a place to check off weekly."

It all seemed so regimented and cold—but what choice did we have?

But I still figured out a way to personalize this rigid system. I'd been just about to get rid of a pair of worn-out flannel pajamas, since they were in bad shape and the weather was too warm for them anyway. Instead, that night, I tore the pajamas into washcloths. If I rubbed the soap on the cloths, I'd be able to take faster, more efficient showers and wouldn't have to worry about dropping that big bar on my toes. I would hand-wash the washcloths and hang them on a drying rope.

That experience certainly makes me appreciate the soft, comfortable soap as well as the washer and dryer in my home today.

I hadn't seen that kind of soap for many years, until a recent walk through an open-air farmers market in France. I passed a large soap stand, and it called to me. And there it was: a huge bar of rough brown soap with some markings on it. "People actually buy it?" I asked the shopkeeper.

"Yes," she said, "it's softer and cheaper than laundry detergent or floor cleaning materials and leaves less residue, so people use it to wash the floors, laundry, and diapers."

As memories from 55 years flooded my brain, I asked her to cut the soap into four pieces; I promised to use it wisely.

I shared the dorm with one girl from Romania and another from Russia. They were okay but not overly friendly. The Romanian girl was an orphan, bitter and angry with life and people in general. The Russian girl was an immigrant, just like me. Her parents were together but they could not keep her. They drove trucks with produce around the country and lived in a trailer most of the time. Here we were, three girls with three stories to tell, sharing the same goals, dreams, and anxieties. What would be next for us? How long would we live there? When would we learn the language and feel comfortable with homework and life?

On my third day there, I received my very first assignment: to collect at least 180 eggs, three mornings a week, from 6:30 a.m. to 9:30 a.m. Kfar Batya not only used the eggs in its own kitchen but also sold eggs to local grocery stores. "I hope you are up for this mission. You start tomorrow," the supervisor announced as he walked out. As a city girl in a country place with no instructions or guidance, I had to make it work.

I walked over to the chickens to collect the eggs, on a bright sunny morning, listening to the birds singing and the sun peeking through white foamy clouds.

Though I enjoyed it when Mom cooked chicken or

eggs, I knew nothing about live chickens and the eggs they laid in their cages.

The first few days, I failed to meet the quota. I was so intimidated by the chickens, running around and controlling their territory.

I was still intimidated and frightened by those chickens running out-of-control around the cages. But one day, all that changed. One bright sunny morning, in a sudden burst of confidence, as I walked into the chicken coop, I unconsciously began to sing the famous "La Donna e mobile" aria from Verdi's opera, Rigoletto. In Romania, I must have seen this opera at least 10 times. That morning, it was playing in my head. Miraculously, while I sang, the chickens walked back to their cages let me collect the eggs without interference. The beautiful music calmed the chickens down! Ecstatic, I met the quota for the first time. Within a few days, I became one of the top egg collectors.

A small action had created a huge outcome. It took me years to absorb this dramatic and growing lesson.

A month later, I was promoted to kitchen helper:

peeling potatoes, cleaning rice, sorting beans, washing the vegetables, and cleaning the dining room tables.

Our diet was heavy on the starch. During self-service lunches, I would pile up a huge amount of pasta, pasta sauce, and a few slices of bread. For dinner, I would have a big piece of chicken or beef or fish. At times, I would look at the chicken and feel guilty, remembering singing to them in the henhouses. But I quickly dismissed these thoughts so I could bite into the chicken leg and satisfy my stomach.

To top it off, I developed an addiction to sweets. When Mom came on her weekly visits, I would ask her to bring me coconut-covered chocolate bars. I'd eat three at a time.

Within six weeks, I'd gained enough weight to make my uniform very tight on me. Was it the carb-laden diet, the fresh country air or my lonely feelings? Probably a combination. Several other girls also put on weight. We overate to feel better emotionally.

On Saturday mornings, we'd eat cold hard-boiled eggs. I often wondered if the child who collected these eggs was going through a hard time, as I had.

And life moved on. We girls would get together on the lawn after our morning prayers and talk. I was learning new words and meanings each week. I was finally making progress and the language was no longer so foreign to me.

School was closed and we didn't have to work on Saturdays, as the whole moshav observed the Sabbath. Saturday mornings after breakfast, we would all head to the synagogue. The first moment I entered the large doors following other children, I felt a sense of energy and purity.

Back in Romania, I used to join Mom for the High Holiday prayers. But this new place felt different. I could touch the air. I felt protected. Yet, at the same time, I felt like a total outsider.

I found I could separate the part of me that was participating from the part that was observing and learning. "Isn't this quite moving and interesting?" I would ask myself. There were no answers. I sat down on the pew close to the window and followed the organizer's instructions.

As the room filled, a huge voice appeared in the

small body of a short young man alongside a young lady. Later on I found out that they were a married couple, teaching Hebrew classes. She stood to the side while he acknowledged our attendance. He said "Shabbat Shalom" and began to read the prayers.

I knew what Shabbat meant (Saturday in Hebrew) but I was struggling with Shalom (peace). Did I have peace internally? Did I experience the emotion of peace? Did I believe in peace?

We opened our Hebrew prayer books and followed the read. That very day was the first time I recited the 'Shema," which translates, "listen, Israel, God is one."

As we were standing and bowing, I felt the jolt of a new way of life in my entire body. Was my mind connected to my frail young body? Was my spirit embracing the moment? Was I even ready for such a powerful encounter?

As the weeks went by, I began to look forward to Shabbat prayers. I began to ask for and inner peace—and I began to believe and trust in the existence of God. It made me feel so much better: less lonely and lost.

Today, I wonder if I would have found my faith

without these moments. Can faith still replace my fears and apprehension? I receive the responses through the choices I make, especially when I tap into my genuine feelings and observations.

I grew with the experience. And after the prayers, I would get on one of the old swings and rehearse my personal prayers and what were my dreams? While at the same time I learned to appreciate and embrace the experience.

Indeed, Saturdays were special. Each week, it was a day of reflection, connection, and learning to believe. Sundays, we'd go back to work, resume our studies, do a few chores in the dorm, and so on.

By May, 75 days after my arrival at the Moshav, I hadn't left the place the entire time and was looking forward eagerly to my 30 day vacation, July 1st to August 1st, 1960.

Friday, we always had a short day, preparing for Sabbath—and Mom always made sure to visit. She would take a bus and walk a few miles every Friday early afternoon. She was delighted to see me, but didn't say much about her life when she visited.

By then, Mom had a job at a restaurant near the main Tel Aviv bus station, making soup and sandwiches for the bus drivers, serving them with homemade pickles and fresh potato salad. It was a survival job and Mom made the best of it. But she always felt exhausted. Each time I saw her, she'd dropped a few pounds, and she looked tired and pale.

The restaurant owner had given Mom a small room in their old house in Yaffa. He had a wife and two boys close to my age. Mom moved her belongings from Yona's house and made space in the closet for my clothes, planning to take a few days off from work during my vacation and travel a bit the country.

But on my third day visiting Mom, everything changed abruptly. We were sitting at the dining room table with the man, his wife, and the two boys. It was Saturday so everyone had the day off.

I wore a light white t-shirt and a short polka dot skirt Mom and Dad had bought back in Romania. I had sandals on and by then my hair was a bit longer. I looked pure, innocent, and my thoughts were inward. I was only 11 but looked older and had a young woman's shape.

While we were all enjoying our meal, the man got up abruptly from his chair, stood behind my chair, and with uncontrollable hands, picked up my t-shirt and reached for my breast.

I instantly jumped to my feet and got outside in seconds. Mom followed me, screaming. My feet flew high in the air just like a dove, I felt the flight and I felt the urgency of the matter. I wasn't prepared for this violation. My body was trembling and my mind troubled.

We got away and felt free. But now, Mom was out of work, we were homeless again, and he had all our belongings.

Mom and I went directly the local police station to report the incident. Still, it was three weeks before we recovered our belongings. And by then, I had to return back to the Moshav.

The policeman asked about our plans. We had none.

Then one of the older policeman offered to let us stay at the fire department apartment right next to the station.

"At least you will have food and water and a small bed to sleep in. You can wash your clothes at night. With this summer heat and wind, they will dry in a few hours." We accepted and stayed there for three days.

On our third day, we decided to walk through the open farmers market and pick up some fruits the sellers discarded at the end of the day. With huge amounts of grapes, cherries, and apricots, we came back to the fire station and shared all the goodies with these incredible kind people. We were also given some bread and cheese and olives. Mom and I smiled; we'd already come far beyond our first day arrival and the junk food awaiting us in the small shikun in nowhere land.

With comfortably full bellies, Mom and I decided to take another walk down the street.

A beautiful girl waved hello to us as we held hands and strolled slowly toward the beach.

I don't know what gave us away, but she turned around and walked over to us, asking in Yiddish. "Are you new in the country?"

Mom smiled. "Yes. How can you tell?"

"I just felt it, the moment I saw you both. You are so connected and yet so lost. Do you have a place to stay?" Her name was Eva. Mom felt at ease sharing a short version of our story.

"Come with me," she said. "We are three girls in an apartment just a few blocks from here. We are new also in the country. I am from Russia and the other girls from Poland. We are nurses. We left our families behind. Now, without permits or knowledge of the language, we are working as escort girls to men looking for our services."

Mom was very taken by Eva's honesty.

"This is life," Eva said sadly. "One day, things will change and we will no longer do this for a living."

Though I didn't understand the language, I somehow knew what she was talking about.

We both liked her. We were saved again, living with Eva for three weeks.

The girls were extremely friendly and very generous. We lacked nothing. They shopped, Mom cooked, I helped tidy up the apartment and cleaned the floors. Gypsies brought us fresh milk, awesome butter, jam, and eggs daily.

Living with the three ladies showed me so much of what life offers—and what happens when we have to make less-than-perfect choices. I watched the girls cry together and ask for guidance. I saw men knocking on the main terrace door and leaving in minutes.

Elegantly dressed and extremely attractive, the girls also taught me all about make-up: the influence of color, when to use which lipstick, face powder and eye make-up. Since Mom used nothing but lipstick, this was all new to me.

Living with these girls showed me how desperation can influence our livelihood. Most importantly, I learned not to judge others harshly unless I'd gone through the very same experience. We never judged them.

Eva told me, "a kiss connects two souls in a shared breath. It's the most meaningful thing in the world. When you kiss for the very first time, remember this. I don't kiss my clients; I leave my soul breath for the man I will grow old with."

Five years later, when I had my first boyfriend, I gave that first kiss all I had and Eva's teachings entered my reality. I still remember the way it stopped me from breathing.

10 years later, I was strolling with my baby on Dizengoff Street in Tel Aviv and stopped for an ice cream. When I ordered, the lady in front of me turned around. Oh, my God, you are Ana," she squealed. "I recognized your voice." I didn't recognize her until she said, "I am Eva.

We both broke into tears, oblivious to everyone else in the ice cream parlor "Is this your baby? Eva commented. You look sensational, Ana."

She too looked fresh, well dressed and at peace. She'd become a nurse and married one of the hospital doctors. "Would you believe I am 37 years old? How is your mom?"

"She is amazing," I said. "Lots of miracles have come along since we lived with you. Mom is married to a great person, and life is wonderful!" We exchanged phone numbers and kept in touch for several years, up to the day I moved to the USA. Her two other friends had gone back to their professions. One married a man in the military and the other was about to get married to a teacher.

I took it all in and I turned another page in my personal experience book. We can paint our lives with our own colors—if we chose to!

But back to August 1st. 1960.

My stressful vacation was over, and Mom and I rode the bus back to the Moshav. By then the police had brought us our clothes. It was a glimpse of abundance, as I packed my belongings Yet, deep inside, I felt poor and helpless.

Mom went back to the city, walking around looking for Help Wanted signs at cafés, restaurants, and hotels.

The very first Friday, Mom didn't visit. Missing the last bus, she called the office and asked them to tell me that she was fine, would come the following Friday, and had a new job. Though I was glad for her, I missed her kind, loving face.

Chapter 2
The Choice

Mom was hired at a successful deli on Rothschild Boulevard in Tel Aviv.

The deli specialized in food to go. They were busy making and delivering chicken soup, stuffed cabbage, meat balls, Hungarian goulash and paprikash and many kinds of salads all over town.

It was Mom who introduced the authentic goulash and paprikash. The owners were elated.

It was a good place. Again, Mom was given a small cozy room above the restaurant.

Mom began to feel good about her position—until a couple of months after she was hired, when the owner asked her on a busy, short-handed Friday afternoon to deliver food to an elderly lady who lived across the street, on the third floor. Mom picked up the bag and ran across the street.

When she knocked gently, a silver-haired woman

opened the door in her robe and searched for a small coin to tip in her pocket. She handed the coin to Mom carelessly, and it rolled down the stairs. Mom just stared at it with a deep pain in her heart.

Humiliated and embarrassed, Mom moved quickly toward the staircase as soon as the customer closed the door. That small coin rocked her world. 'This is not compromise,' she told herself. 'This is settling for something so much less than what I am—and who I am.'

The minute she went back to the deli, she resigned. In an hour, Mom packed her belongings, received her last paycheck and walked out into the afternoon heat— homeless and jobless once again.

Scary though it was, she felt liberated and emotionally cushioned at first.

But as she walked down beautiful, tree-lined Rothschild Boulevard, fear replaced her courage as she sat down on one of the benches, feeling overwhelmed and depleted—and began to cry uncontrollably.

An elderly man casually reading the newspaper on the next bench heard her cry. Then he noticed her small suitcase. Slowly, he placed the paper under his arms and walked over. "I couldn't help but listen to your cry. It sounded terribly sad and deep. Is there something I can help you with?"

It took several minutes for Mom to reply. She told him the story of the coin rolling down the stairs: the tip that stripped her of her dignity.

He listened intently as she shared with him some of her other life stories.

When Mom stopped talking, he waved his hands above his head. "Listening to your story, I have an idea. First of all, you need a permanent home for you and your daughter. You need to shine and not dry up like an old rose. I want to introduce you to someone."

"Someone," Mom repeated.

"Yes, he is my neighbor, a widower for several years. He has a seasonal business and he is a good, hard-working man with a lovely home in a great area of Tel Aviv. He has grown children. He is looking for a good woman, a wife, a partner who will be there for him and grow old with him.

"He is around 65. And you?

Mom was in her mid-forties, and she replied with a smile.

"Great! He is in good shape. How about tomorrow, I will arrange a meeting between the two of you in a local coffee shop?"

With hope in her heart and trust that the moment called for a brighter day, she thanked him—his name was Manny—and took the bus to Yona, my cousin, explaining to him the chain of events. Yona wasn't too excited but he asked her to come in and gave Mom the same room we stayed before to use and chill for a while.

The next day, Mom put on her best clothes. Wearing a pleated off-white skirt, silver sandals, and a striped top with navy blue, beige, and red colors, she went straight to the meeting café and sat down next to the two men.

She and Itzhak hit it off instantly. They conversed and they shared and they laughed and cried at the same time, as if they'd been lifelong friends.

Five months later, Mom married this wonderful man in a quiet civil ceremony; Manny was the only witness. That very day, Mom came to the moshav to give me the news. "Pack your things. I am taking you home," she said. "You will love it!"

I was astonished by this huge event in my life. The other girls looked at me with envy and wonder.

We took the bus back to Tel Aviv. And when we arrived to our new home, Itzhak, my new stepfather, opened the door with a huge smile and a warm welcome.

The house was a standalone home with two entrances— one each for the main house and the backhouse, where Itzhak had a business. There was a huge balcony and the street smelled and looked spectacular. And it was only a block off Dizengoff Street. Overwhelmed, I timidly and gratefully explored my bedroom and the adjacent bathroom.

It was a miracle. And before going to sleep, I sat down on the edge or the bed and prayed to thank God for my blessings. Within minutes, I fell asleep.

The next morning, Mom and I walked over to a private middle school. Mom enrolled me into 6th grade and I was ready to embark on a new journey.

Who could believe it? We'd gone from rags to riches

in a few days! One event, one connection, and one determination had changed the course of our lives. I was lucky to attend private schools. Mom bought me the finest of clothes and life was sweeter than honey.

Speaking of honey, Itzhak had many bees in a different location, where the honey was made, but he kept a big inventory of canned honey in the backhouse. He had regular customers buying his delicious natural honey.

Indeed I still remember the first bite I took, digging with a small spoon into the jar. It was delicious—and so was our new life.

From that day on life took many turns and twists, but things almost always worked out for the best. After the honey-tasting day, another even more precious day happened 10 years later, when I gave birth to my only child, Sean, at age 21.

Who can describe that moment? It was a celebration— but it caused a health crisis. After a long, tough birth, I had stomach hernias, severe pain, and lots of other complications. I lost my appetite, dropped 20 lbs. and kept getting weaker and thinner.

My then-husband got really worried. We visited several doctors before finally meeting a surgeon from Switzerland, who was the first to give us hope.

"Let's do surgery," he said. "I cannot guarantee, but I believe once we get inside, I will know what to do. You might lose your belly button—but what is a belly button, when you deal with life?"

The day before the surgery, I felt troubled and restless. I took a walk from Mom's house directly to the ancient synagogue on Allenby Street. Memories of the milkshake and so much more entered my busy mind.

But as I walked in, I felt a deep, enriching silence. No one was inside and no sounds penetrated the stillness.

I breathed in the deep spirit of the place and allowed myself to relax into a feeling of buoyancy. My little voice said, 'it's you and me, Ana. God's presence and all that you want to share and express.'

I began to cry. Not a sad cry, but one filled with hope and faith.

I turned to God and asked for only one thing: "Please give me years to see my son grow up, enjoy grandchildren, and have the opportunity and wisdom to give something back to the world. No matter what, God, I will not complain or get upset, test me and test me again and I will show you that only one thing matters: Life!"

I kept my promise and God granted me my wish. The surgery was a success and I gave up on my belly button. No bikini on the beach. The tradeoff was wise.

I cannot begin to tell you how many challenges I had to overcome since that very moment of prayer and plea. I went through tough times, riches to rags, rags to riches, countless homes, and a few marriages, even starting all over again in yet another country.

But look at me. I am giving back. I write and I express. I share and I give and am happy and grateful for the gift of life—and your presence in it.

From chicken eggs to prime rib. From a small job to running corporations and serving organizations as CFO, CEO, COO, VP of sales, and VP of relationships.

Yes, ultimately it's all about relationships: how we pursue them, build them, and nourish them.

My life had its ups and downs—but I would not trade it for anything else.

The choices we make are the pathways to the directions we take and the results we achieve

Chapter 3
The Sound of the Guitar

When Sean was 17, I took him to Spain. It was my first time visiting this amazing country.

One highlight of that delightful trip was attending a Flamenco show, watching enthusiastic dancers move to the strong sound of several guitars playing in harmony, long into the night. I absorbed the music like a wave of warm ocean waters.

We visited the open market in Barcelona, ate lots of pizza (since the local food did not agree with us), drank lots of fresh juices, and enjoyed the rich salads.

And we took in the amazing Modernist art of Barcelona. I still have tremendous respect and admiration for the creativity and passion these artists manifested, devoting their lives to a world filled with exuberance in design and emotions.

At the end of our trip, I returned home to California. But Sean flew to Paris to look at colleges and explore the city. As we waved good-bye at the Barcelona Airport, and headed to our respective gates to meet our flights, I could see my son walking away, feeling mature and adventurous.

But like any mother having the first big separation from her child, my heart sank. Still, I knew it was the right thing to do. I had to encourage him and empower him to pursue his goals and dreams—to discover his own world.

When I arrived back home, Mom and my son's father ganged up on me with a barrage of questions and accusations: "Why did you let him go so far? You could have said no. Sean, my son is too young to travel the world on his own!" my ex-husband declared

But the one that influenced me the most was my mother asking, "What kind of love do you have for him?"

"The kind that loves unconditionally," I responded. "The one that does not place any blame or guilt on him! The type of love that understands and honored one's individual dreams and inspirations." But neither of them were ready to hear that message.

Sean and I spoke frequently during his month in Paris,

and the time passed quickly. The City of Lights, a city of love and beauty mesmerized him. Yet, he chose to come back and enroll at a local college instead.

With great relief and elation, my heart lifted back to calmness and joy.

Thinking about this at the time and later, I had to ask myself some big questions:

Was it love to lead him to independence and self-esteem? Would I have been more loving to make his choices for him?

At the time, it all felt so clear and understandable. But now that I have teenaged grandchildren eager to follow their own dreams, those exciting and scary questions are rushing back at me like a fast train.

Even though it caused friction with his father and my mother, I still feel I made the right decision to let Sean choose his own path. And as the time approaches when his children have to choose the school and career that most appeal to them, I hope he will give them the same freedom that I gave him.

I was always pursuing my career; my identity and my

personal goals and dreams. But now, once again, I find myself in the crucible. I ask myself: Where did the years go? What are my goals? Where do I want to go next—and with whom? At times of crises, those goals and dreams became pale and unimportant.

But as soon as I pick myself up again, I keep on going, keep on believing, and keep on knowing that each and every one of us has a purpose, laced with faith and direction.

And I also ask myself questions about those younger family members. How will Sean and all the other empty-nesters manage when their children have left? How do they fill the big void? Do parents just pick up and downsize and move away from the familiar nest to a whole new place? Is such a dramatic change necessary for their survival and sanity?

Have the couples become foreign to each other? Do they still have the spark? Is the connection weak and fragile? Do they only talk about their kids' lives and never about their own accomplishments and dreams? Will fear, worries, doubts and loneliness fill up the new space? Is someone there to listen when they lose direction and shout out in desperation, "What are we going to do?"

The good news is that we can control much more of our lives than most of us think we can. Just as we can create and sustain our bodies and our external shapes, we can shape our lives. But it's easier said than done.

I knew people who gained tremendous weight following personal and family changes. Others became narcissistic and focused only on themselves.

There is no judgment or blame here; each of us is an original. We all have to not only discover what feels right for us, but how to stay on track, even if others make different choices.

Chapter 4
No Boundaries

Do we need boundaries to live a healthy and happy life? I will let you answer that.

For me, it works both ways. The wrong boundaries may hold us back from experiencing, exploring and exhaling deeply.

But other boundaries are guidelines that discipline us to walk on—and ultimately balance— life's tightrope, skillfully and happily. Think about listening to yourself when an experience stops feeling good, and how many problems we avoid by staying within our internal boundaries. And also think about the thrill of successfully going beyond your own artificial comfort zone to achieve something magnificent.

Kids, especially teenagers, need boundaries: that fine and gentle type of discipline they desperately seek and yet also resent.

Let's explore some of those boundaries as examples that we might apply and acknowledge in our life journey.

Parents might set certain rules at home as boundaries to keep the children more in sink with schoolwork, athletics and social connections. For example:

Johnny, I prepared a list of chores for you to do the following week:

1. Please take out the trash before pick up date
2. Organize your room: separate clean clothes from dirty clothes
3. Place dirty clothes in the hamper
4. Wash your clothes once a week
5. Place clean clothes and shoes in the closet, where they belong
6. DO NOT eat in your room
7. No more than 30 minutes of TV after school
8. Assign an hour a week for talking with us (parents) without any distractions, phone, TV, or any other gadgets

9. Filter before you speak

10. If someone offers you drugs or alcohol, ask yourself, is this good for me? What's in there for me?

11. Choose your friends

12. Choose activities that bring you joy

The list may go on and on. You get the picture.

We as grownups also need some boundaries, such as...

- Live within a budget

- Put aside funds for yearly vacation

- Listen before your speak

- Dress for success

- Eat what's good for you

- Drink what makes you feel better

- Choose the proper time for exercise

- Get enough sleep

- Make time for your loved ones

- Surround yourself with energetic people

- Eat at home more often

- Keep a clean home (less clutter)

- Keep a clean car

- Keep a clean mind (breathe in and out every few hours)
- Attract what you desire
- Don't flirt with your best friend's significant other
- Keep your passion, love, and intimacy for your partner
- Travel alone only on business
- Break away from phone addiction
- Plan for home parties
- Go out of your zip code and have fun
- Have only one or two drinks at the restaurant
- Eat small portions and listen to what your body is asking for
- Exercise regularly and choose the plan that best fits you

So what really happens to us when we exercise certain boundaries or keep a good list of all that we want to achieve, accomplish and embrace?

These boundaries will extend your life span; the fences you build around your own spirit and soul and emotions will keep the darkness away.

They're not about keeping you locked up with your emotions. On the contrary, these boundaries will contribute to your freedom and self-expression. They'll help you discover what you're all about—and understand that the world doesn't only revolve around you.

When you become more centered and together, you influence everyone around you—and the world becomes a happier and more connected place.

When you have a purpose, when you feel totally liberated without any side effects, then you know you're on the right track.

Yes, you might stray away from the main road occasionally and take a detour down a bumpy side road.

Often we don't think of the consequences. It's easy to get carried off in a storm…to want to belong, be part of the team, follow others even to the wrong places. It's tempting to forget about the outcome, live in the moment and enjoy the highs and lows without asking questions. And that's when our lack of boundaries can get us into trouble.

But the solution is simple: learn to check in with your intuition. Your instincts will get sharper the more you let yourself trust them. Just tune in to the desire and see if it is really worth following. If your instincts tell you this is an outstanding opportunity to x-out the impossible and allow you to be you, then follow this new passion and explore where it takes you. But if your gut tells you this is crazy and won't help you, step back.

Chapter 5
Where Do We Go
from Here?

One morning, doing my usual getting-ready-for-work routine, I looked in the mirror and didn't recognize myself. I turned down the second light in the bathroom and asked myself, 'Who is this person looking at me kindly? What happened to the face I was so accustomed to? Where did these extra wrinkles and tired eyes come from?'

Glancing at all the expensive wrinkle creams on my counter, I found myself reflecting on the size of the skin products market: over a trillion dollars, with skin rejuvenation, eye serum, peeling creams and so many other products ranging from $10.00 to hundreds of dollars.

I'd tried pretty much all of them, as well as various nutritional and anti-aging products.

So why weren't these products working? Yes, I could try plastic surgery or Botox. But the real question is, where did that face go?

Like most people, I'd picked up a line or a wrinkle for every stressful moment, glimpse of sadness, choice to let something go, change of partners or job or home, and all the rest of it.

With all my experience and study of life, I've learned to brush off unpleasant thoughts, clear my head, shift to happy and joyful thoughts, filter choices—and just go on with life as if nothing happened.

So I made a decision to stop trying to hide my age. I can still look and feel young by wearing young-looking clothes: fitted shirts, colorful t-shirts, long and short dresses, attractive shoes—and by using hardly any makeup—just lipstick and a little mascara, nothing else.

I chose not to cover up my face anymore. My wrinkles mark wisdom and a life lived fully. They are badges of honor, and I feel cleaner and less overwhelmed.

Youth has been gone for quite some time—so why am I so bothered by the reflection in the mirror?

I got my answer quickly. That I didn't want to accept reality. I wanted to go back to the illusion that I can look youthful and energetic.

I felt the fight taking over me—unpleasant and emotionally disrupting. I began to breathe heavily. Anxiety took over within minutes.

Now, I had to deal with that too. But I realized that the key to shift away from this unfriendly attitude was just accepting that at this age, I can still look terrific—but I won't look like a woman in her forties or early fifties, and I shouldn't pretend to.

Feeling better about my looks but still a bit wary, I got out of the bathroom after putting on some lipstick, mascara, brushed my hair carefully, and walked over to the closet where my clothes were waiting for me.

Years ago, I started preparing my clothes, shoes, and accessories the night before—so in the morning, I don't need to worry about searching for an outfit. I listen to the weather and get everything ready the night before, saving time and hassle.

I put on my clothes, shoes and belt. Then I went back to the mirror and looked again, with open curiosity. 'What do you think now?' The reflection inquired.

I stood there mesmerized for a while. Then the right answer came to me:

'Okay, I am ready to embrace the new day. Just as I prepare my clothes the night before, I can prepare myself mentally and emotionally to greet the new day, starting the night before.

That great idea made me smile as I walked downstairs to my garage and got ready to drive to work.

As I got into the car, I thought again about that crucial moment when the person staring at me seemed so unfamiliar, causing feelings of sadness and confusion. Perhaps that happens to you sometimes.

A few days later, I made a conscious decision and gave away most of my skin care products. After all, they contributed only partially to making me feel beautiful. For me, it has to be all the way—or nothing.

It's a relationship we build with the person inside of us. Instead of dressing up spending hundreds of dollars on creams, I choose to dress up as a person who has a voice, something to say, valuable lessons to offer—and smile like a 30-year-old.

Let's join forces and make the best of the new day.

Keep it that way and continue the ritual day after day.

We will get used to it. Eventually we'll stop thinking or counting the wrinkles.

After all, both Carl Jung and the Kabbalah (Jewish mystical text) tell us that before you turn 40, life is just practice.

At 40, you become more aware, more awake, and more realistic about all those little moments navigating your feelings.

These life experiences, both before and after 40, led me to develop and practice The DOXA Method, A SUCCESS formula transporting your fears into success.

****

SECTION 2
THE DOXA METHOD

Chapter 1
Find Your Passion, Spirit, Purpose, and Connection— the DOXA Way

Wake up! Open your senses! Free your eyes, ears, nose, mouth, and fingers to explore the magic of this (and every) moment. It's time to discover your passion, purpose, and spirit—and let them shape everything you do at home, at school, at work, and everywhere in between.

I want you to love your life, the way I love mine.

Loving my life, with its many tumultuous transitions, wasn't easy or quick. I'm a double immigrant who started from nothing, twice—and had quite the checkered career. English is my fourth language. I had to learn how to immerse myself in happiness even when things seemed desperate.

I'd like your journey to be shorter and easier. Let me show you the way, and shortcut the many painful twists and turns I had to take. I'll share with you the best success formula I struggled to understand through years of trial and error, years of failing and getting up again.

All of us can learn to wire ourselves for success. Yes, even when life seems like an endless series of unexpected and frightening challenges. We can still choose how to respond, and our choices change the outcome.

My Best Success Secret: The DOXA Method

The best success formulas are simple—because simple formulas are easy to remember and easy to make a part of your life. The DOXA formula, one of my favorites has only four steps:

D – Desire

O – Outstanding

X – X out the impossible

A – Allow you to be YOU

We can put this into practice in every part of our lives—into all life's puzzles, mysteries, and desires. As we focus on these four steps, we transform thought into action and create the life we choose.

You might feel that you have no control over your

life—that you didn't choose your situation. And truly, there will be some parts of your life you can't control. But even when he was a slave in a Nazi concentration camp during World War II and had no control over his circumstances, Viktor Frankl refused to relinquish control over the inner person he really was. If he could do it under the worst circumstances a human being can experience, we who live in freedom can certainly do it as well. So yes, you will have unforeseen challenges and complications— but they don't rule you!

Let's start by thinking about all the parts of our life we *can* control, all the places where our choices make a difference.

For example, we can choose to...

- Eat healthy, nourishing foods
- Get a good night's sleep
- Exercise our bodies every day
- Hang out with friends who encourage our greatness, not our passivity
- Take steps to achieve a meaningful and well-paying career

The list goes on and on, at every step from infancy to old age. We strengthen our good choices by acting on them. Think about this traditional fable:

An old Cherokee is teaching his grandson about life. "A fight is going on inside me," he said to the boy.

"It is a terrible fight and it is between two wolves. One is evil—he is anger, envy, sorrow, regret, greed, arrogance, self-pity, guilt, resentment, inferiority, lies, false pride, superiority, and ego. The other is good—he is joy, peace, love, hope, serenity, humility, kindness, benevolence, empathy, generosity, truth, compassion, and faith. The same fight is going on inside you—and inside every other person, too."

The grandson thought about it for a minute and then asked his grandfather, "Which wolf will win?"

The old Cherokee simply replied, "The one you feed."

Through the DOXA Method, you'll feed the good wolf. You create the kind, gentle, and loving empowerment to ask yourself questions, sift through your responses, let them marinate, and improve your answers through your actions.

You'll find after a while that you get clear answers that you can convert to action—and that you're using both sides of your brain: tapping into both logic and emotion. And it all joins in harmony to create a life you can love.

Choose Authenticity!

My first challenge to you is to live life authentically and genuinely. Authenticity gives you the strength to face those puzzles, mysteries, and desires—and come through any obstacles stronger than ever.

Using the DOXA Method, that authenticity can transform your thinking. If you've been stuck in fear or negativity, DOXA will help you shift to the positive thinking that embraces and accomplishes your goals. At the same time, you're not a slave to your ego. You recognize that humility will get you to those goals much faster and on far more sure footing than arrogance.

Life is a series of choices. At any moment, we can be asked to choose. Perhaps you're planning a vacation. You'll choose where you'll go, how you'll get there, who's coming with you, what sort of place you'll stay in, and many other decisions.

Someone could ask, "Will you marry me?" If it's someone you have grown to know and love, you'll at least consider saying yes. If it's a stranger you met 15 minutes ago in a bar, you'll probably choose no. But maybe you'd choose to invite that stranger to have coffee and get better acquainted when you're both sober, and two years later, you answer differently when the question comes up again.

Every time we make a choice, our opportunities shift. Some doors open while others close. You may start to regret some of the choices you made, some of the doors that closed. Just remember that 1) other doors opened when you made that choice; 2) sometimes, as in the wedding example above, you can revisit the situation and choose differently; and 3) even if you can't revisit the choice, you have new and exciting possibilities at every moment. Never let regret be a weight around your neck!

Owning the Choosing Process

When you choose in a conscious way, you own the choosing process, and you make stronger, better choices.

Pause your routine and take a break. Take a deep breath and ask yourself: What are my choices? What path should I walk on? Is there a sign in this? Do I need to shift to another path?

Connect and tap into yourself. No one knows you better or understands you deeper than you do. Honor yourself and your personal identity.

As you bring that choice into balance, you'll be amazed by the results you create. You'll experience a complete domino effect that improves many areas of your life. When one area is balanced and functional, everything else falls into place.

Better yet, it doesn't have to be perfect. Perfection can be a roadblock that keeps you from moving forward—because the time isn't right, because you want to sharpen your skills, because you don't have your team in place... Because, because, because. Don't let all these "becauses" become your excuse for staying stuck. Start down the path!

Unless you're doing brain surgery, flying a commercial jet, or doing something else that actually requires perfection, you just need to get moving. There will be plenty of time to improve it later—and meanwhile, you can begin to experience the joy of knowing you're doing what you came to this life to do. Even if it's not utopia, learning to love your life and fully appreciate it is still enormously satisfying. Better yet, your positivity will be contagious; you'll attract interesting, compassionate people who can help you. Never again will you have to feel isolated, alone, or robbed of opportunities.

Come and be part of this magical journey! The rest of this book will show you how I work this magic in my life, and how you can, too. And we'll keep coming back to and going deeper with the things we're talking about right here in Chapter 1.

Let's get started.

Chapter 2
Sweet Tastes of Life!

Now that you're living and practicing THE DOXA Method, you're stepping away from fear and entering the new gates of success and happiness fueled and guided by Passion, Spirit, and Purpose.

There is nothing like it. Once you experience this magical way of life, there's no going back.

Through the DOXA Method, we learn to:

- Be at ease with our hearts
- Develop a dialogue with our minds
- Ask questions as freely as we wish for, and
- Find the responses through the choices we make.

With the DOXA Method, we expand and stretch our minds. We blend our thoughts and actions with our hearts and emotions. And our possibilities become unlimited.

People often ask me to write my entire life story and share my thoughts, feelings, and experiences.

My life has been exciting and challenging as long as

I can remember. It's been full of unusual circumstances, challenges, and wonderful outcomes: the dramatic highs, lows, and everything in between. I've shared this story in detail in my earlier book, *The Money Flow*. So here, I'll just give a quick overview of the highlights and concentrate on helping you develop a positive, empowering outlook and philosophy. I'll ask you questions about what you might choose to keep sacred, help you experience the sweet tastes of life, and so much more.

When I was not quite 8 years old, I got scarlet fever. My town, Cluj (the capital of Transylvania, Romania) was infested with scarlet fever that winter. Hundreds of children ages 7 to 12 were sent to the hospital. Most of them shared rooms with other children and healed pretty quickly.

But not me. I guess I was special. My scarlet fever was so strong that I was given a room by myself. I was an only child, and living in that single hospital room was punishingly isolating. I will never forget that lonely time.

I had no one to share my feelings, my fears, and my dreams with. I had no TV or radio and no one to talk to. All I had was myself: my hopes, my dreams and my reality. It was a lot to hang on to. I was three weeks in that small room and three more weeks at home recuperating from this terrible disease.

Yet this isolation may have been the most growth full period of my life. At first, I asked questions like "Will I ever get out of here? Will I be healthy and go back to my regular activities? How is this event affecting my mother?" But as my illness continued, I became comfortable with all that I was feeling. I accepted my circumstances and felt that hope was on the horizon. And after more than six weeks, I was able to return to normalcy.

What was my normal life? Sharing a bedroom with Mom in a small apartment on the 3rd floor of an old building, with a large bay window overlooking the street. We had a tiny cooking area and shared a bathroom with 3 other families.

Every week, Mom purchased us tickets to the movies from India, opera, theatre, ballet or classical concerts. Yes, I was raised with culture, music, and deep emotions.

I felt love, compassion, kindness and co-dependence.

My parents divorced when I was 5. With no siblings or large family, Mom and I got very close and made the best of the life we knew.

Is There a Role for Prayer?

Throughout my childhood, I saw Mom mumbling a few words here and there. But I never associated this with praying or spirituality.

This is one of the things I want to explore with you—and remember, for all the questions I'll ask you throughout this book, there are no right or wrong answers. There's only what's true for you, right now. Your answers may change later on.

What is prayer to you? Do you pray? Do you think of what the future will bring to you? Are you stuck in the past? How is your present time—school, career, family, work, social, and your intimate life?

Do you often forget about who, how and why you're here in the first place?

I've forgotten numerous times in my life. Sometimes, I had to place others first—and got consumed by the need and the task. Other times, I acknowledged another person's vulnerability of the stressful situation, and I had to take action and take charge. I'm sure you can relate.

Let's go back to the "I"—the person inside of you. Get to know that person! Understand and be just with yourself, even if feelings of guilt, overwhelm and inner emotional pain take over.

A song, a tune, or a place might remind you of a connection, a lost love, a sense of belonging and often, the desire to go back and do it all over again.

That's where the impossible comes in. Regardless of how much you want to run away or deny the inner seed, you cannot escape reality.

So, let me ask you a few big questions:

- Is realty connected with the illusion?
- If so, how?
- If not, are they two separate facets of life we need to keep apart?
- Are we living in the present time, forgetting the past, and not worrying about tomorrow?
- Are you still absorbed in past experiences, feeling the sweet tastes of life? Or do you simply just build?

- Do you embrace a mysterious, uncertain future without worrying about how it's all going to play out?

At first, living in the present may sound like something important to do—but consider that maybe it's not. We achieve so much more when we let go of the past, extract wisdom and seeds filled with experience, and dream about what we want to accomplish in the future.

The "Time Zones" and life cycle

For a long time, I've been fascinated with the three "time zones" (past, present and post time (future) I accept that these time zones play a significant role in our lives. Despite our efforts, we cannot change the cycle and influence the circulation of time.

Let me return to my mother as an example. Mom is over 100 years old and in declining health. Her mind is rapidly passing through, her body is too tired to function. She barely sees what's around her. Most of the time, she lives in the past. Little speckles of tomorrow and the present poke through, but they're totally skipped and forgotten in minutes.

Comparing what she used to be and what she is today is incredibly powerful; it reminds me daily that all of us are fragile and mortal.

Mom is in the process of leaving this physical world—leaving me. Despite the care I give 24/7 and all my love and appreciation for all that she has done, for all that she ever was, and all that she ever gave—nothing can alter this destiny.

All I can do is continue to be there for her, love her unconditionally, and accept this turn of the clock.

Why is it all going by so quickly? I wish I knew! But when we're young, we are filled with expectations, desires, and actions. We overlook getting older, until we finally realize that each and every one of us will get there, one way or another.

We pray and wish for long lives, getting old with loved ones around us, and not suffering or being a burden to others.

We ask for so much!

Is Mom suffering? I don't know. She never complains; she smiles a lot. But the reality in between the smiles shows a grey picture, painted in feelings.

She is a true hero to me, holding on to a frail, fine thread that connects life as we know it to what we truly don't know—what we often fear and keep as an unknown sacred mystery throughout our entire lives.

Shifting between watching her and my own routines, I've learned to feel time, and not just fill time. I share this phenomena with people all over the world. The concept is well-received but not steadily followed or practiced.

I don't know how this works for you; for me, it took more than 30 years to shift and navigate and let go of past moments, peel off the onions filled with experience and dress up again in the present time, keeping illusions and dreams alive in my daily routine.

These dreams keep me going when the sun decides to hide behind the big heavy dark clouds. When no one calls me or cares to hear how is my life going. When I feel lonely and sad and depleted—and especially when I go deep and accept that "time stops for no one, not even for me."

Time: Feel It and "Goal It"

Do you ever feel lost? I sure do! I get lost in the feeling, lost with emotions dancing around me, and lost with the worry that I don't have enough funds to do all I hold dear—from travel to donating without limits to heal this troubled world.

Both in my own business and in the company I work for, I've been blessed to achieve success. Almost 10 years ago, while working full time as a consulting CFO for a manufacturing company in Gardena, California, I began writing and selling books and offering lectures, workshops, and group coaching.

A decade later, I'm still doing both. I love working with numbers and keeping organizations alive and prosperous—but I've reached deep within and tapped into a whole new creative world that I cherish and feel passionate about. I'm driven to share my wisdom, my tools and my findings with the world.

Rather than just waiting for the big break to influence my life, I'm actively enabling it. It's been taking much longer than expected—but I still haven't given up on it.

Instead, I chose to give more of whatever the situation—or the person—demands. I clean up the soil before planting new seeds. I stay away from so-called friends, spend time with real friends, and I'm content with my three times zones. When I experience a setback, I just move on and move forward.

Sometimes, I cry when no one sees me—when I feel that I cannot change the situation or the relationship. It's no longer up to me, and I let go. I recognize that the current situation is fully orchestrated by the Universe— and that everything is exactly where it belongs.

But I also cry when I feel a certain joy in my heart, expressing my gratitude for a new day as I say the Morning Prayer: welcoming the newness and the unfamiliarity. I simply build my enthusiasm around hope and love.

Why is it necessary to feel time? Simply because when we feel time, we learn to appreciate it. We can experience the joy of all that we can accomplish with the time allotted to us.

We cannot exchange time or do anything else with it except use it (to act, but also to contemplate) or let it slip away. But we can embrace and dwell in the time we have—a behavior we must exercise.

When I joined the working world, I was only 10. In

my sixties, pursuing several businesses of my own while working full-time in corporate finance, I made lots of money for companies and their owners. I was instrumental in helping these companies grow and sustain themselves. Since our society defines success in financial terms, I am an outward success.

But I believe whole-heartedly that each of us defines success for ourselves. One size never fits all. To some people, its education; to others, travel or making a difference in the world. The list goes on and on.

For me, my real success is that I have also empowered individuals (including many business and nonprofit leaders) to shift fear into faith. Through this work, I create not just success, but also happiness and contentment.

Facilitating this transformation lets me feel liberated. I love the person inside of me! I keep busy and I am thrilled beyond words.

Yet, I still have plenty of unmet goals. I desire to:

- Be debt-free with a lovely home of my own, with a summer house close to the Mediterranean
- Have a good assistant

- Travel a lot
- Conduct workshops around the world that empower people to find joy in their career and build both their personal and financial success
- Embrace each and every day with passion—with elevated spirit and purpose.

This is my desire, my world, and my identity. I cherish it each and every moment as I follow my purpose and believe in the good of it all.

Without purpose, we are empty, searching souls. Discovering that purpose is the guiding light that gets us through the commotion and busyness.

50 Years to Climb Out of the Pit—

But You'll Do It Much Faster

In my youth, I didn't start as the happy, fulfilled person I am today. It took decades. By sharing my journey, I hope your path to joy will be decades shorter than mine.

Let me take you back in time and you can see what it was really like.

My relationship with Mom was as close as it can be. Even as a small girl, I felt the co-dependence and often worried about what would happen if she was no longer with me. I had NO answers to those questions.

I was so scared! As a child, I never lived childhood. I was a serious young girl, crushed under this burden of fear.

Mom didn't know any other way to help me banish fear. Neither of us was good at letting go, being less co-dependent. She had difficulty focusing on her own life and identity. It was hard for her to accept that we are different and that we pursue different goals and intentions.

It was just her way. Without family, father, or siblings, I was searching for love, for connection, and for independence.

My journey helped me find all three of these ideals—but still, I felt something was missing.

Finally, at 50, I felt an inner shift. I did not need this or that. I was finally complete! I could learn and teach. I could transform challenges into opportunities. And I began to experience a totally different life.

Can you imagine it took 50 years to get there? 50 years of learning, listening, and low self-esteem.

I had no confidence before reaching 50. I constantly doubted my deeds, dreams, and desires. I was a total introvert, shy and insecure—a lost soul.

Often I'd felt a bit angry. I even blamed Mom for all my failures. But eventually, I learned that we must take responsibility for all that we do, all that we feel and all that we experience.

The guilt, the shame, and the blame took hold of me at age 20. I was married to a very nice serious man, who loved me totally and unconditionally. But I didn't love him the way young women love their significant other. I cared about him but I expressed tremendous selfishness throughout our relationship. I was so totally self-absorbed that I became unfaithful. I was still just 21 when I gave birth to my only child, Sean.

He is quite amazing and accomplished. At times I can see he is too somewhat troubled and consumed by questions. I can only acknowledge that he is the only one who can answer those difficult questions for himself.

I went through several divorces after my first one. Looking back in the mirror of truth, I'm just now realizing that these dissolutions occurred simply because I did not love. I just did not know how, why, when, and where to love.

It appears that the only people I can truly love and cherish are my mother, my son, and my two grandchildren. They are the beacons of light in my life and I only feel the closeness, the family love, for them.

What a discovery!

A few years ago, I married again. I admit that often when I expect love, kindness, devotion and fun, I feel lost, depleted and withdrawn into my own soul and spirit. My husband and I can feel far apart sometimes. But the lessons I learned from previous marriages provide me tremendous guidance and patience and the desire to make this marriage work.

It does take work; there is no utopia. But with shared intentions and love, I know we can make it work. In the past, I chose not to do that work and gave up too easily. This time, I hope I've learned to stay and explore the tensions, to find ways of being together even when it might feel hard. I recognize that this is true of every long-term relationship between equals—and now, finally, I value and understand that.

I'd always associated love with new relationships: the chase, the pursuit, and the new experience. Once it becomes a way of life, a steady connection, a routine—I've tended to lose interest and chase other avenues. But now that I recognize this hurtful pattern, I can stop it. If I feel the old discontents rising up, I can "stop, look and listen"—and work with my husband to resolve the issues, instead of running away from them.

So where am I today? I'm free at last. I don't feel ashamed of my life experiences. I don't feel co-dependent on anyone. And I know precisely my desires, passion, and purpose.

It's a great place. I want to bring millions of people to join me and feel and embrace life.

It's all intertwined and connected to time and our deeds.

Sometimes I wonder: is Karma extending my success, accomplishments, and dreams?

Perhaps!

Through the turmoil, through the so-called bad choices, and through the pain and the sorrow, I've learned that no one is perfect.

So what makes me entitled to teach and empower people to transport fear into success and reach happiness? It's intertwined with my lifestyle and how I see the world. I do not judge.

Living in the three time zones is a revolutionary discovery. It leads directly to contentment, accomplishments and an authentic life worth living.

Who Are You, Really?

So who am I? The answer goes well beyond our names. We generally introduce ourselves by our names, and maybe our titles. But that's only the tiniest piece of who we really are.

In many Native American cultures, people earn their names based on their deeds. Thus, in the movie, "Dances with Wolves," Kevin Costner's character was called Dances-With-Wolves because he'd been seen wrestling a wolf. His bride, Stands-With-Fist, earned her name when she stood up to a group of tormentors with her fist raised.

What if we introduce ourselves as?

- Kind

- Giving

- Sharing

- Smart

- Experienced

- Loyal

- Deep

- Spiritual

- Sincere

- Intelligent

- Hardworking

- Educated

- Generous

- Energetic

And the list goes on and on.

Where do you fit? What are your names? What qualities would you like to exude—and be influenced by as you bring grace into your life?

Remember, first impressions count. They impact the whole relationship.

You can dress up and sometimes take off names. But what is the core of your essence? How free would you like to be? Can you see yourself living a balanced and happy life?

Daily, I share my names with the Higher Power. And I ask my Higher Power, "What fits me today?" and the message comes on loud and clear.

Today as I write this, the answer is "curious." I'm curious about how much this book will resonate with you. Will you be asking questions like, "Who am I going to grow old with? Will I travel the world without financial worries? Will my grandchildren and their children be proud of me? Will I love the way I always wanted to love someone close and dear to me?" Tough questions—but someone has to answer them.

I am not referring to infatuation, chemistry, sex and intimacy.

Pure love is the essence of total giving, total commitment, and total devotion.

But sometimes, we have to get our nightmares out of the way first. And that leads us to...

Chapter 3
The "Lost" Nightmare

Let me tell you about a disturbing dream I've experienced at least once or twice a week for years.

I used to wake up with a cold sweat and sit up in bed trying to make sense of it. And although I was happy that it was only a dream, it was far too close to my reality.

The dream is always fairly consistent. I am in an unfamiliar city/town. I go down to purchase something like a book, stationery, or just something to eat. And I can't find my way back to my hotel or apartment.

I get lost. Regardless of how carefully I memorized the place, my destination is changing on me. I'm overwhelmed beyond words. I panic; total anxiety and fear set in as I acknowledge the simple truth that I don't know how to get back.

Sometimes, I ask people crossing the street. But they can't help, leaving me even more agitated.

Anxiously, I conjure up one crazy idea after another to find my way back. I clutch my purse, which contains lipstick, a comb, my wallet with some cash and a few credit cards. But I have no cell phone or any gadget to connect me with my friends.

Wallowing in self-criticism, I rage at myself: why did I leave at all? I was safe until then.

Finally, I wake up to my much better reality, and look at all the things in my bedroom. I feel relief, but I'm still drenched in sweat after the scary nightmare.

While I'm thrilled that it was only a dream, a fiction, an illusion—I keep asking myself why I have the same nightmare over and over again. I get up tired and overwhelmed.

This dream has power over me. It jogs my entire soul and spirit to wonder, to ask, and to find out what it means. What is this dream teaching me? Is it a sign?

I've come up with many possible answers:

- It's about emotional awakening! It's about finding myself and getting to know myself after all the years of battle.

- It can also be about choices, about following my dream and waiting for answers to come. About reality replacing illusion and fiction.
- I get it, but the dream still represents a powerful jolt in my life. I work very hard not to get consumed by it and choose to let go.
- Yes, I'm in the midst of waiting for my choices to bear fruit and my efforts to materialize into a new and better day-to-day reality.
- In the meantime, I'm in the process of lighting the fire filled with illusions and hope—and I just wait.

I've learned tremendous lessons from this dream—especially from connecting my feelings with my logic and common sense.

As a creative person, my creative juices flow smoothly within my reach. But at the same time, I need to adapt and adjust daily to and pursue all that my reality demands.

Is it easy? Is it workable? Is it productive?

Sometimes it is. But occasionally I too get stuck in a place where I lose my patience and anxiety takes over. *When will the big questions be answered?*

I love to work and produce and feel independent and active. But I wrestle constantly with questions like:

- What would I like to do for the rest of my working life?

- Where?

- When and how will I sustain myself?

With all these questions bugging me, the only way I reach peace of mind is when I put my hands together and express my trust, my faith and my attitude towards the so-called bright tomorrow.

When I wake up in the morning, I greet the day with a smile. What does this day promise? What will this day deliver? And how is this day different from the other days I experienced.

When I treat it as a surprise, all is good. Calmness replaces chaos.

So why am I sharing all of this with you? It's because it's your turn to ask yourself some questions:

What are your dreams? What's inside your head when your dreams feel so real and so overwhelming? Do you dream at all?

These questions are a direct link to deeper questions that can help you develop your own philosophy. Here are a few examples of those deeper questions, and my answers at this moment.

1. Can you name 5 powerful emotions that influence us daily?

   Here are my top 5 (your list may be different):

   • Love

   • Worry

   • Anger

   • Judgment

   • Blame

2. Now let's list 5 tangible areas where most of us are challenged:

   • Family

   • Friends/lovers

   • Money

   • Home

   • Career/education

Again, your list might be different from mine. Select the ones you find most meaningful.

3. What happens if we connect one of the emotions and one of the challenge areas?

    Let's try:

    - Love and family
    - Money and anger
    - Judgment and friends/lovers

    Examine them! Blend them in your mind. See where is this all going?

    Do we love for the sake of money and comfort? Is reality breathing through us, or is it an illusion?

    If we choose a career simply because of the influence of a close family member, have we chosen well?

    If we cherish and adore our lover and share amazing experiences together, yet our friends tell us how wrong he or she is for us, do we heed their advice—or stick with our soulmate?

    Where do we go from here?

    Life is a blend of reality and illusions displayed in

color. But too often, we choose the black-and-white, sterile approach—only to discover that we chose temporary comfort over long-term growth.

Where is your home?

Where do you belong?

What are you searching for?

Do you smile from inside out and know deeply that it doesn't make a difference to you who listens?

Can you thrive without others' approval?

Chapter 4
Meditation

For quite some time, I knew what meditation meant. But I couldn't get myself to do it.

To take a few minutes out of my busy day and simply listen, be still, and connect—it felt almost impossible.

Didn't I have to keep busy—doing and thinking at all times? To STOP all of that was totally foreign. It was not only unfamiliar but also unwelcome.

Until one day all of that changed.

I'd been sitting outside my office, taking a break and eating my homemade meal, when I looked up at the sky and observed dark clouds moving in. It was wintertime in Southern California and like many others, I'd been wishing for the rain to come.

My immediate reaction was "finish your lunch before you get soaked!" But suddenly I felt a strong urge to put my plate down on the grass and look up into the sky. I put my hands up and a deep quietness took over. At that moment, I remembered a passage from the movie, "The Tempest," which I'd watched often. Playing the part of Prospero, the actor Raul Julia asks, "Give me the magic!"—a plea for storm and rain. Oddly enough, at that very moment, I experienced a deep calm. It was my first meditation, and I continue to meditate daily since.

I take a few moments and stay still. I listen to the birds singing, to the wind blowing through the leaves and to the sound of the universe telling me that there is so much more out there left to imagine and experience.

It's a chance to welcome the beautiful world: the newness, the change, and the calmness.

Through meditation, I learned how to close the busy, loud outside world surrounding me and focus on what I need to do, desire to do, and love to do. I close off the outside world and keep to myself—and to all that I choose to express, feel, and write.

Fortified by meditation, I even tuned out the noise of my co-workers and my surroundings enough to write several books amidst that background of sound and noise.

In the process I grew taller: not in height, but in

understanding, observing, and acknowledging that life is everything.

This very deep and sincere awareness leads me beyond mere existence. Now, I live each and every moment with love and appreciation.

Do you meditate? What kind of meditations seem right for you? When do you meditate?

Are you at peace with yourself? Do you know who you are? And what you are?

These questions aren't intended to burden you or stress you out. Please treat them as extremely friendly, sympathetic to all you're experiencing at this exact moment. But understand that not only are these skills important, they're also something you can learn.

Like any of us, you can become a leader, you can become a strong person, and you can become loving. But no one becomes any of those overnight. Either we choose to learn and get where we want to go, or we're born with a notion that drives us, and through our life experiences, we acquire the skills we need. We feel and smell the fruits of our labor—and are filled with love for the gift of life. Similarly, you can learn to meditate, or even to pray.

How About Prayer?

Do you pray daily? Do you find a place where you feel that even the air around you is dancing to a soft tune you can hum and sing to?

Prayer and meditation are totally related. One can exist without the other, however, by doing both, each complements the other. And you can raise the bar—and the positive results—as high as you wish to.

Let's go back for a minute to meditation. We learned that meditation is simply taking a break from our busy routine and overwhelming lives—going to a place of stillness, breathing in and breathing out calmly, rewarding our spirit and soul with a fine and delicate recharge.

People practice (and benefit from) various types of meditation all over the world.

Prayer is quite different than meditation. It rises on a scale you can only understand when you're not a stranger to prayer—or when you're ready to embark on this journey.

Meditation is a phase of interconnecting, an inner space helping us get deeper and deeper into the person we claim to be and appear in the world.

But prayer is an expression, a connection to a higher power with whom you feel comfortable and at ease. No one should attempt to convince you that you must pray in a religious format or any other setting defined by others. You can pray in the middle of the desert, on a stormy ocean, in between large trees in a huge forest—or outside your office door, on your patio, or in your living room or bedroom.

The place is yours and only yours. You want to connect, you want to ask questions. You want to share something very dear and intimate. You want to feel the relief and the answer to what is on your mind, spirit and soul.

You might want to ask for something that you've desired for quite some time: a better career, a baby, a new home, a trip to an exotic place, more love in your marriage, even losing weight or finding the courage to make a change (among many other possibilities).

Is there a connection between meditation and prayer? Absolutely! As you meditate, you learn to connect with that inner person living in you; you also find more peace and strength to connect with the higher power. You're vulnerable and humble—and you feel great about it. And you become less intimidated, less scared and less worried.

I've asked many people to share their thoughts and feelings about meditation and prayer. A few claim that meditation is an interim step that leads to the higher frequency of prayer. Others said that prayer actually led them to meditation.

What are your feelings? Your perception and your reality?

Fear and worry occupy a huge place in our lives:

- How will my life turn out?
- Will it be successful, or filled with doubts and desperation?
- Will my partner always love me?
- How will I look in 10 years?
- Will I have enough funds to retire some day?
- Who will be there for me when I need the support?
- When I am sad and troubled, will one of my friends listen to my plea?

These questions are natural and totally realistic. Prayer reduces the impact of turning to others and co-depending on others: What do they say? What do they think? What do they recommend?

You are not an island. You do need humane connections and support—but reducing co-dependence empowers and leads you to the answers to all those questions.

I don't know about your inner life—your prayers, your connection with the inner you, and the power you feel at home with. But let me take you to an experience going back more than 44 years.

That day was rainy. The wind was howling and darkness was about to fill the sky deeper and deeper. I was hurrying to my parked car, wanting to get home as soon as I could to my little baby boy (he was 3 at the time) and my mother, who babysat for me that afternoon. My husband was working late and riding the bus home from work.

The weather conditions mirrored my life—and my feelings of sadness and restlessness.

As I got into my car, I closed the door quickly and

turned on the ignition and the radio. But I just could not make myself take off. I was in the driver's seat physically. But emotionally and mentally, I wasn't ready; I felt self-pity and unease.

Suddenly, I felt the presence of a higher power. I began to cry and with no questions asked, I wrapped myself in its strength. I stopped crying. And immediately, I began asking myself the big questions: Are you happy with your life? Do you want to make a change? Do you feel alone and isolated?

My answer came quickly and clearly: I had to change my life. Eight months later, we were on a plane to the USA to follow an old dream and start a new life. We sold everything we owned: a condo with no mortgage, a car that was already paid off, furniture, china, rugs, decorative items, linen, toys, books, and albums…all we had.

We'd expected that we could easily replace all these belongings in the USA. As it turned out, that was an illusion; it was years before we dug out of our new-immigrant poverty.)

I was 24 at the time, energetic, full of life and filled with huge plans.

The next day, I woke up finding myself praying. I asked for peace of mind and to find the warmth kindling my spirit and soul. I had to drain my entire being to reach within and accept who I was—*and who I could become.*

You can also reach that peace of mind, that place of comfort. If you want it deeply enough and you are authentic and genuine about it, you'll discover it just when you expect it the least.

Since age 7, I've visited many places of prayer all over the world. Entering some gave me the chills. Others made me feel I was being embraced by strong physical arms in a big hug. A few greeted me with just a hint of spiritualty and calmness.

I recall one of the first of these visits so clearly. I went to a church in Cluj with my dear neighbor Margaret, a devout Catholic. Soft voices joined in lightly with a rumbling organ to enter my light young body. Although I was only a child, the feeling was mature and far-reaching.

I didn't know the song or the meaning of that tune. But it was so powerful that I stood still between the columns and began to understand that we are just visiting this planet for a time. We don't know what happens after this visit. But we can choose to believe in something that suits our soul, giving us peace and admiration.

On another visit, to an old synagogue, I heard no music. But as I sat down on one of the old pews, I felt the presence of thousands of people's energy, the desire to live, the passion for love and the purpose in their entire being.

Who was there before me and who will be there many years from now, sitting on the same spot, perhaps feeling my heartbeat and my love for them?

No more questions asked. The answers are the questions transporting us from fear to happiness.

We change. Life follows.

* * *

On the holiest Jewish day, Yom Kippur eve, the Day of Atonement, Jews traditionally greet the special fasting day with humility, wearing canvas sneakers (to be comfortable and to avoid wearing a dead animal skin—leather) and white clothes for purity.

The Kol Nidrei prayers in Aramaic announce this

magical moment. Each and every year, regardless of the place or the sound or the chorus following the hymn, I get teary-eyed and moved to the smallest molecule in my body.

Kol Nidrei applies to every living human soul on this earth. We are all included in this very moment, whatever our race, religion, social status, age, education, etc.

We are one on that night as we recite the Kol Nidrei three times, recognizing its power and recharging in that moment. Kol Nidrei is considered the holiest prayer in all of Judaism even though its text (releasing us from all vows we might make in the coming year) opposes a key principle of the religion. According to some traditions, this is because when we release our vows, we are asking G-d to reciprocate in kind. If G-d made an oath to bring harsh judgments to the people in the coming year, we ask G-d to release these vows and instead grant us a year of happiness and redemption.

Prior to the Kol Nidrei, we pray the Hazorea le Tzadik: planting for the righteous (which says that G-d will provide for them): When we plant the right seeds, most of the time we reap the fruits—a far greater bounty than we'd planted.

I cannot find anything more powerful, more universal and more inspiring than this humble prayer.

I was told by my mother that my grandfather had the honor every year to recite the Hazorea Letzadik. Indeed, what we plant, we reap. The choices we make are the answers to our questions.

Planting is not easy—but it's beautiful, in every shape or form.

My grandmother Hani, whom I'm named after, was a sensationally sweet and bright woman. Every Saturday at noon, she would serve lunch to a group of ladies who would bring her their questions and troubles. How cool was that? I never met her, but I feel her presence in all my speeches, my lectures and all the kind and generous words I place on paper.

It's probably not a coincidence that her name sounds just like honey. I believe there is much more to a name than just the name literal meaning—and that names have power.

Chapter 5
Relationships

Let's start this chapter with the most important question: Do you have a close and loving relationship with your own self? No matter what your life circumstances and opportunities, the person you see in the mirror is part of that journey.

This is a huge question. I often wonder why we invest so little effort into getting to know, accept, and enjoy the person living inside of us.

It's not easy to do so. It's easier to focus on everyone else and everything else besides this. It's less complicated and less emotional.

We need to acknowledge our debits and credits, the deposits that bring us a high return, and the withdrawals from our personal emotional bank account.

When we create and build a healthy, open, free relationship with the person inside of us, we open ourselves up to create and build amazing relationships outside the circle of "I": with our partners, siblings, children, grandchildren, friends, colleagues, neighbors, lovers...even someone we meet in the grocery checkout line or sit next to on a bus.

Relationships are the pillars of our mental, emotional and physical being. We cannot withdraw ourselves and live a life of exclusion—unless we seek depression, bad health, destructive relationships, and self-sabotage.

Attempting to withdraw from others can wreck our work, education, career, social life and everything around us. Ultimately, those who choose withdrawal end up with no self-esteem, no confidence and nothing to show for their lives.

Please don't go there!

This word, "relationships," reminds me of so many splendid moments when I felt that the world was colored in rosy shades and everything was complete and beautiful.

These moments were so alive! When I've been open to others, I felt so good about myself, all that I did, all that I aimed to accomplish. And, looking back, every lesson seemed valuable and positive.

Validation is key to all relationships. Are they easy? No, not at all.

We find ourselves out of love—or out of lust—when we realize that the connection has faded away. Without the connection, communication flies out the window. We become two strangers missing the thread that once deeply connected us—and wishing for something totally new.

Why is this happening to so many of us? And more than once in a lifetime?

Where did we go wrong? Was the course meant to last only so much time? How much did we really love that person?

What made us click originally? Why do we now feel the disconnection? Why do we think separation will solve the problem we have…or choose to have…or simply believe we have?

Some divorces are quite a shame. The relationship could have worked out if only we'd validated the other person, kept focusing on all that meant something to us, and communicated our feelings and our emotions directly. Make time for the important things that now seem so insignificant; as an example, always look at your children's faces. When you have them in your life, just observe their expression. It says it all.

At times I wonder who is more mature, the kids or us grown-ups.

We're supposed to act like mature people—but we don't. We blame, we're angry, and we judge everyone else while fearing to reach deep inside ourselves.

There is no perfection out there—and there is no life without storms.

We can pick our battles as they say. We can gain strength and courage and move in instead of move out.

Yet, in some cases the separation is necessary and totally useful.

When and how do we know the difference?

STOP EVERYTHING YOU DO!

Meditate

Pray

And you will get the answers.

It's quite a journey going inwards—and it's a must.

You consider it all. But how often do you only consider the person inside of you and no one else?

Relationships demand compromise and lots of giving. If you're not open to it, don't go there. Plenty of people choose to have no commitments, no strings attached and no plans together.

Because of my own very mixed record, this chapter is very close to my heart and my soul. I've had some amazing relationships—and some very weak and short-lived ones.

I choose to settle. Other times, I compromise. And on other occasions, I have to get away, get out, and start fresh.

Did it work for me? I wonder at times.

Ultimately, the key is learning to care for yourself, to be gentle with yourself and with your emotions. Choose the people you want to be surrounded with, have lots of fun, and enjoy each and every moment.

The rest is whatever you want to make of it.

Everything in life requires a relationship of some sort. Relationships take shape and grow when we learn a simple formula: give, listen, take, offer, and care.

There are 5 steps to successful relationships of any kind: personal, intimate, or in business:

- Pursue the relationship
- Engage in the relationship
- Define the relationship (or identify) the relationship
- Nourish the relationship
- Validate and appreciate the relationship

This is it!

Chapter 6
Tradeoffs

For most of us, our lives are a series of trade-offs. As an example, we might chose to purchase a home far away from our work and commute several hours round-trip. The home is much cheaper than closer homes. But ultimately, we don't consider our energy, the stress of driving a busy freeway for hours a day, the gas, the wear and tear on the vehicle—and our short fuse when we get home to our loved ones. And then the next day, we repeat the same pattern again.

Or we move far away from our family and close friends to accept a better-paying position on the other side of the country or continent.

Sometimes, the trade-off is less obvious. We eat sweets to compensate for unmet emotional needs—a depleted sense of being unloved and unappreciated. We gain weight and fall into the same cycle over and over again. Some of us even make trade-offs when choosing a mate. We put aside our values, our core being, and our livelihood to make a commitment to a financially strong person who is not healthy to be with.

I could list hundreds of other examples.

Where did our values go? Didn't we know any better? Weren't we taught not to go that way?

Of course we were! But we did anyway. Some part of us thought, 'why work hard when we can replace the stress with the "easy life"? But where did that choice *really* get us?

Who thought about it? We asked no questions.

And here we are again, standing at another intersection of life: lost, drained, a few years older, and perhaps wiser, too.

Not all the trade-offs are negative and disappointing. However, we often make these choices without acknowledging the real life-altering consequences.

I had a lovely neighbor years ago. She was of German descent and loved her two German Sheppard dogs.

I never saw any guests or family members visit or any type of socializing in her yard or home. After a few years living next door to her, I wanted to hear her story. So one day, I gathered enough courage to ask her, "How long ago did you move to this neighborhood?" This is what she told me:

I moved here 10 years ago from the East Coast. I simply needed to change the course of my life. I had a few siblings but they moved to Florida for the warmer climate. My children are all grown up and they chose to dismiss my parenting and love for them simply because I left their dad. He was an alcoholic, and I could simply take no more of his behavior.

My son and daughter judge me. Even today, they think that I could change his drinking. But I could not.

So here we are. I visit my siblings in Florida three days every two years. And I am waiting for the day when my kids will call me or just show up at the gate.

I have one friend who is not very well so I go see her once a week, bring her some good German salami. My dogs love me unconditionally. I worked as a teacher and live off my pension and Social Security. They provide me a good lifestyle and I am happy.

I am approaching 68 years young and I ask for nothing else.

I live a simple life and that's it.

Her story entranced me. The next week, I invited her for a meal. She was grateful, showing up with a home-baked cheesecake.

We continued to exchange pleasantries until the day I moved away. I said good-bye and wished her all the best.

She had traded her values for a husband who was not good for her—and when she finally reclaimed her identity, she found herself estranged from her children. But I don't judge her harshly. Who can judge?

The business world is built on trade-offs. We constantly trade various commodities for other commodities. Even today, we barter one product or service for another, or for money.

Trade-offs can also be about waiting for the right

moment to fulfill our dreams. While it's good to dream big, we must actualize those dreams in ways that don't sabotage our own future.

My Russian-born stepfather, Itzhak was a practical man. He grew up in a small, loving family—but very poor and totally uneducated.

When he turned 21, he made a huge decision to emigrate from Russia to Israel in search of an easier and abundant life. His parents approved.

He had no money or profession but he was ready to do any task and work hard to survive and progress. And that was plenty to start his new life.

At first he was a horse and carriage driver. After a year, he got a job in a factory, where he met his first wife. They fell in love and got married in a simple ceremony with 5 people attending.

After their first son was born, times got tougher. He purchased his own horse and carriage, thinking that on his own, he'd generate a higher income. But often, he barely had food for the horse and food for his family.

He told us that some days he just cried and prayed. He

was often hungry—but he continued to believe that one day life would get easier.

On a bright sunny spring day in Tel Aviv he walked the beach searching for work. He walked for miles and miles. All of a sudden, his moment of desperation and fear lead to a successful idea:

'The beach needs places for visitors, not just to walk but to sit down. People need a place to sunbathe and parents need a shady place to watch their children play and swim. I will design and construct beach chairs and matching small beach umbrellas for all the beachgoers,' he thought.

And so he did. He got a permit from the city and built a workshop in the back of an old building. And he began to build chairs, made of wood and colorful nylon, with adjustable sun hoods.

Customers showed up and it was a lucrative business. Itzhak rented the chairs eight months of the year. During the four months each year when the business was closed, he repaired chairs, he painted them, and he made sure that he had enough inventory for the upcoming season.

A seasonal business run by a seasoned, creative, and inspiring man.

The beach chair rentals provided him and his wife and three children a good life. Itzhak bought a lovely house in a great neighborhood.

He was the man Mom married when she and I were homeless and destitute shortly after emigrating from Romania. He rescued us and life was sweet.

His story always touched me and taught me how to think clearly.

On rainy winter nights when he would just look at me and simply know what was on my mind, he loved telling the story of his youngest son, who married his lifelong love at 21. She was a teacher and he partnered up with a relative to purchase a machine shop and produce airplane parts.

When the couple got married, they were eager to spend all the money they had on an elaborate honeymoon. They came to Itzhak and shared their dream vacation plans.

Itzhak listened deeply. "So what do you think, Dad? The son asked.

"It all sounds great and fun." But then he continued. "You leave and you come back. So what then?"

Itzhak's response sounded cold and unemotional to them. But as they headed home that evening. It all suddenly made sense. "Dad's right. Let's build a life here and get established. We will travel and see the world when our feet are planted wisely and safely. We are only 21—and life is just beginning for us."

So instead, they went camping for a few days and afterwards back to work—and back to their loving union.

They have two children. Their son is an airline pilot/ engineer and their daughter practices law. They traveled extensively for many years. Last year, they took their children and grandchildren on a long cruise to celebrate their 60th anniversary.

The only one thing we definitely cannot tradeoff is TIME. There is simply no price tag for it. But sometimes, we use our time most efficiently when we delay gratification for a while.

Chapter 7
Travel—and the
DOXA Method

How do you feel about traveling? Where do you travel? What do you think and feel about how you manage your time away?

In this chapter I'll take you back to the beauty of time, the power of time, and the true reality of time.

You've heard the expression, "living in the now"—the present time. There's no time like the now.

Researching the existence and quality of time, I've discovered that we all live in the three time zones (past, present, and future) at all times.

As time moves forward, we let go of time passed by, we act and embrace the very moment—the now, the present. And as the clock moves forward, we get a taste of the time coming our way and all the things we can look forward to.

Letting go is the toughest part of the circle of time. The

more we learn to let go, the more we can focus on the now, take action in the now, and develop a positive attitude towards the unknown future.

Please look at the clock design on the cover of this book.

I purposely chose the red color to signify letting go. The toughest action we must take, it also warns us to absorb and recognize the circumstances.

The orange middle circle is the present. The more we practice letting go of the past, the more we are present in the now—and the more we feel accomplished.

The dark green circle of our future is in the center. Although it's the smallest circle, it is the heart of the entire new clock. It reminds us that yes, we live in the three time zones.

The DOXA Method and You

Remember the DOXA formula I introduced back in Chapter 1? Now it's time to make it an everyday part of your life. A welcome advisor and guest, or even a family member.

The DOXA Method connects and links the three

circles of time. It allows you to wrap time, life, and your feelings together. It leads us through the three time zones.

When you focus on something that will make you happy in the future, you pull yourself out of your daily routine and ongoing stress. It relieves you from the lifetime of constant obligation dangling over your head.

Wrapping together the past, present and future, the DOXA Method lets us extract the seed from the three principles:

1. Attract
2. Believe
3. Create

Each of these three principles reinforces the four steps to the powerful DOXA Method. As you'll remember, they are:

- Desire
- Outstanding
- X out the impossible
- Allow you to be you

Where would we be without time and without the desire to succeed—to transport fear into success? And why am I using the word transport? Because, using the DOXA Method, we can actually turn our fear into something positive in our day-to-day lives. We can recognize it, allow it to be there, and transform it. How? By befriending that fear: letting it reveal its purpose—but not letting it control us or keep us from acting on our own deepest purpose. So we can learn from the fear without getting paralyzed by it.

Then the fear becomes one more tool to help you achieve the success you desire for yourself—that intimate desire you so cheerfully live with.

Yes, when you travel with time, the DOXA Method becomes a natural part of your existence. Time travels— and so do you.

The DOXA Method will enhance the travel and help you rotate through the three time zones. You'll learn to turn the wheel steadily, safely, and successfully.

On another note, travel adds to our knowledge of people, our understanding of places, and our appreciation for their beauty.

There is nothing more rewarding than travel— especially if you're raising children or seeking personal growth. I had a moment many years back, as I visited Florence, Italy for the very first time.

I got so mesmerized by the beauty of the city that as I stood in front of the **Filippo Brunelleschi Cathedral**, admiring the architecture and listening to the voices of many languages—I caught myself wondering if it was a real moment or an illusion.

A few years later, I went back to Italy. This time, my mother, my son, and I went to the Amalfi Coast.

"Why is the pizza so wonderful here?" Mom asked one evening as we were sitting at a round table in a small restaurant in Sorrento. I didn't know exactly why—but we ate pizza almost every day for the rest of our vacation.

That week was more than magical. Mom was just about to celebrate her 75th birthday in Italy. My son was 21 at the time, old enough to order a drink. I was 41 years old.

Looking back, we all feel that this trip will always be one of the highlights of our lives. We walked, we talked, we smiled, we shared and we ate every meal together for 10 days. I wouldn't trade that trip for a billion dollars.

The experience will never go on sale.

And that brings me to another question: Where would you like to be in three years? Five years?

Does that question feel overwhelming? Let's rephrase it: Where would you like to be in 3–5 years, emotionally, physically and financially?

That should be easier—because it's more concrete. The first question, without the three areas to cover, was too vague, too abstract. You could have answered 100 different ways. But they would all have a little war inside your brain, so if you're like most of us, you didn't answer at all until I gave you something specific to work with. You can use this powerful lesson in how our minds work to form and achieve the goals that move you forward— starting with your answers about your goals in those three areas.

These are not easy questions. But they're essential. The answers give us thoughts, feelings, and direction. The three facets are totally interconnected and intertwined; you can't separate them out.

Your answers to these questions shine a light on your

own choices, your personal outlook on life, and your ability to follow your purpose.

Here's where passion, spirit, and purpose fall in place. The DOXA Method activates our minds as it moves time forward—and forward again.

You're welcome to write the answers directly on this page. Or choose a note pad, your laptop, an audio recorder, your smartphone video, or any other tool. How you record your answers is not important, as long as you record them.

Whatever your answers, they belong to you. You own them. You have a right to shift them or navigate through them as you feel is right for you.

Since it may help you to see another person's answers, I'll share mine in the chart below. I'm delighted to spark your own answers by letting you see mine.

If you'd like to share yours, please visit http:// doxamethod.com/3-year-goal-questions and fill out the easy form you'll find there.

	Emotionally	Physically	Financially
3 Years	Happy and balanced.	Fit, healthy, and full of energy.	Own several properties and travel around the world.
5 Years	Happy and content. Travel the world.	Attend my grandchildren's graduations. Fit, energetic, healthy. Keep the same weight.	Successful— financially secure. Save and give away as much to charity as possible.

This is how I feel about these questions today.

Tomorrow, my specific answers might be different. But I will always aim to be healthy, fit, and energetic... passionate about life...elevated in spirit...and focused on a greater purpose.

10 years from now, I might live in a different country most of the time. Your goals and priorities will probably also shift in ten years—but let's leave this out for now.

Three-to-five years is a good framework for planning an overall sense your emotional well-being, your physical well-being, and your financial status.

Always remember that these three are deeply interconnected. Interestingly enough, each of the three components influences the turning wheel of time.

If we are not available emotionally, our mental health and physical health are impacted deeply. The negative impacts on mental and physical health will also interfere with our financial status and our financial strength and security.

And yet, if we focus only on financial security—if we choose to live a life focused on money instead of mind—our outward financial strength will be an illusion, built on sand. If your emotional, mental, physical, and spiritual health are not intact, your financial well-being is at risk of crumbling at the first unforeseen circumstance. The bad decisions in other parts of your life could ruin you financially, too.

Let me wish you phenomenal success with your

three-to-five-year goals. I'll be so proud of you as you turn your best dreams into reality.

And this deep and sincere chapter leads us to the next chapter of this book.

Chapter 8
What Would You Change, if You Could?

I ask people across all careers, ages, and different geographical locations one simple question: "What would you change, if you could?"

Why is this question so important? Why must we ask it? Why must we answer it?

Why? Because this question empowers us. It shows us how to embrace life. By answering, we can filter our next opportunities and choices. We begin to see clearly, feel deeply and act independently—and to build a path to change the parts of our lives that aren't working for us.

It's all about how we feel and how we think. And how we blend feeling and thinking to create the life we desire.

The first time someone asked me this question, I was 26—and I was astonished. "Why are you asking me this? I don't want to think about it now," I responded.

But I did think about it.

That very day, on my commute home, I felt disturbed and emotionally weak. I was moved and I felt it.

It made me feel terrible. 'What is this? A balance sheet with debits and credits? A pencil and eraser? Perhaps a marker?' I wondered.

As I was driving, tears rolled down my face—fogging not just my vision but my thinking. I repeated the question to myself. And as I neared my house, I had a massive awakening. It was a powerful moment I will never forget.

Yes, I wished I could have changed a few of my choices—absolutely!

Why? Because those choices had negative consequences that still affect me decades later.

We can't change the past. But we can change how to react to it, and what type of control it has over our lives. I had to learn to let go and "reboot."

That kind of letting go opens up a huge opportunity to create positive change in our lives. When we learn to let go of past emotional burdens, we also accept our choices as the best they could have been at that time, in that situation. Over time, our answer to that key question loses its power to torment us with guilt or shame.

You might even discover that some of your choices have created a happier, more productive life. For me, they've led to the small family I love so dearly…the friends I cherish and appreciate…all the skills I possess…even to my ambition to live the best life I can while finding ways to enrich the world.

Our choices and our opportunities are servants for life. These choices—even the hard choices made under difficult circumstances—shape our lives and contour our moments. They allow us to grow, to learn, and ultimately, to teach.

A life without tears, without the sensation of feeling lost and depleted, is no life at all.

The painful moments, the despair, and the longing for something different represent the seeds we plant over and over again.

Time cultivates and nourishes the seeds. Whether the fruits you choose will taste sour or sweeter than honey, it will still be a taste you can choose to savor, apply and share.

All of us want to feel fulfilled. We want to have a good

life, a long healthy life. We're always uplifted by love—and that love replenishes itself whenever we give some out.

Some of our goals will materialize and some will not. Whether or not a goal works out, take a minute to ask yourself (non-judgmentally) why: what did you do or not do that helped bring about this outcome? How might things have turned out differently if you'd made different choices? What external factors or circumstances contributed to the way things turned out?

For me, this set of questions always leads to growth—but especially when I ask myself about a goal I failed to reach. What did I learn from these disappointments? How can I be an instrument for others to reach their dreams more often and more?

The dream I shared with you earlier often takes me to a place where I ignite my feelings over and over again—and give thanks for them each and every day. I'm grateful for the time I circulate in this mega world. And with each movement, I still practice letting go. I focus on what positive and happy deed I could do in this moment—and what I'd love to achieve tomorrow.

At times, fear enters my mind and tries to take over the thought, the feeling and the choice. I sit with it for a while. "Why are you here," I ask silently?

"It's habit from long ago," the fear states firmly.

"I know," I say, "but there is no room for you in my life."

"Yet," fear insists, "if I didn't show up, how you would know the differences between strength, courage and fear?

Now, I start to go deeper. "Yes," I agree. "Welcome. But please don't stay too long. I have gained my courage and my strength not to give in to you. Instead, I want to give more. I have so much I can share."

And slowly but firmly, the fear begins to drop away as I deliberately replace it by revisiting my accomplishments and embracing future success.

It's quite normal to feel and experience this constant internal trial.

Fear and worry are right there when you least expect them, buzzing in your ear as you grapple with questions like:

- Does he really love me?
- Is she the right one for me?

- Am I a good leader?

- Could I take another course to learn more?

- Should I move to a place with more opportunities?

- Will I lose weight with this program?

- Will aging slow down for me—or will it slow *me* down?

We must transport fear to face it—and then diminish it.

By transporting the fear, we naturally become unresentful. We stop fearing the fear itself; we no longer feed it or give it such a high value.

We can trade fear for success! This is healthier and more likely to succeed than trying to reach success by transporting fear to where it' is most potent.

We are wired to feel fear. And certainly, some of our fear is justified and totally applicable.

However, other times we obsess over fear, even when it's totally illogical. Just like anxiety, it can be over the smallest molecule of circumstances.

Chapter 9
Is Passion Inherited?

Let me share a bit of my family history—not to brag, but because there are lessons in it for you.

For My Father, Clothes Made the Man

My grandfather wanted my dad to be an architect. He had a passion for building and design, and he hoped that Dad would feel the same way. But that wasn't the story. Dad had a passion for fabrics. He wanted to make something special out of the various fabrics he purchased as a young teenager at the textile shop.

So battle after battle ensued. Finally, after a huge fight and some mutual disappointments, Grandfather Irwin relented. He sent my Dad off to Switzerland to study at the very top school for clothing design.

Dad felt great about the venture. He knew he could achieve his goals, because Irwin was wealthy and owned buildings, businesses and horses. He ran the largest lumber company in Hungary, expanding to Czechoslovakia and other countries.

So Dad left home for Berne and Basel, Switzerland to study clothing design.

He loved it. And he fell in love with Switzerland.

Dad lived in a beautiful apartment overlooking the river in Basel owned by his Father and he had plenty of funds in his account.

He got married in Switzerland and had a daughter. In 1943, they moved back to Transylvania, then part of Hungary (now Romania), where both his and his wife's family lived. Unfortunately, that was not a good time to be a Jew in Eastern Europe. All three were captured by the Nazis. My father survived first a labor camp in Russia and then Auschwitz, but his wife and daughter were killed in a concentration camp.

After the war, Dad continued his passion for designing special clothing for men. Government officials, doctors, lawyers, and successful business owners ordered their suits and topcoats from him.

And when my mother was liberated from the camps,

she traveled to the area to track down her brothers. She was told about a skilled tailor in Cluj, and she met and married my father. I was born in 1949.

Although he sold his business and put his faith in Communism in the postwar period, my father's work was exceptional. He taught me the differences between fabrics and how to judge fabric quality.

Mom was not so enamored of Communism. Political differences and other issues led to their divorce in 1954. But my father was still a force in my life until Mom and I immigrated to Israel in 1960. The next time I saw him was 19 years later in 1979, when I visited Romania with my then-husband and son. It was an emotional reunion, and turned out to be the last time I saw him. Dad died in 1983.

Recently, I remembered him clearly as I went to pick up a few alterations from my favorite local tailor in my area. There was a man getting his pants shortened. Bartan, founder of Classic Tailoring smiled patiently, marking the work with his chalk in his hands.

Of course, I thought of my father and all the clothing he'd marked during his lifetime. Watching Bartan reminded me of how much I appreciate the art in making a garment fit perfectly.

And it reminded me that one size DOES NOT fit all—in any part of our lives.

Just as we choose and tailor garments, we need to feel and choose what fits us best and suits our spirit—in personal relationships, in work, in our view of the world, and more.

Life is like fitting those garments. We mark the areas where we're vulnerable and sensitive. Then we either cut off the pieces that are hurting us to the core or fold them inward and make the best of the end result.

Cutting off is a way of letting go. And through our journey, we find so much to let go of.

Some things we need to let go of are the size of small pebbles, like the ones shinning on the beach when summer is in full force. But others are giant boulders. Each was something we once held significant and dear.

With every inch of breath, letting go is the beginning of a happy fresh start. Yes, you're ending a certain relationship, custom, feeling, or familiarity. But now, you can be free to grow and blossom—to wear the beautiful, comfortable clothing that was made just for you, in your size, to fit your style and your shape.

From Vintner to Scholar

What about my mother's family?

My maternal grandmother was part of the aristocratic Eisenstaedt family, which still leaves its mark on the region. They even had a big castle. They were scholars, and writers.

My maternal grandfather came from a prosperous family running large-scale wineries and farms. They owned hundreds of thousands of acres filled with tremendous vegetables, and fruits.

But after my mother was born, her father's land got flooded. So, with a huge pain in his heart, my grandfather sold the rest of the saved land and retired at 44. He divided the profits among his sons so they could pursue their dreams and start businesses of their own. Business had been his passion. But starting over at 44, he committed his time to studying ancient Jewish religious texts: the Talmud, the Torah and all the ancient books. He occupied his mind seeking answers to his questions. He spoke at various events, wrote, and was always available to solve problems and relationship issues.

From his story, I learned that it's never too late to start over, that hardship can be overcome, that letting others feel heard and understood is some of our most important work, and that success can be intellectual or emotional, not just financial.

Please keep the many lessons I took from my grandparents in mind as we head to the next chapter.

Chapter 10
CHANGE—and Changes

How often we try to resist or escape change! With all of our being, strength, and mind, we throw up one roadblock after another. And the faster that change approaches— and the more dramatic its impact—the higher and thicker we build those walls.

But the change is cosmic. And change is guaranteed. As the clock ticks, time has already moved from yesterday to today—and is already speeding toward tomorrow, bringing change along.

Change is part of our lifecycle and lifestyle. We need to not only accept it, but embrace it. Only then can we make change our friend, shape a future that's better than our present.

As I write this, I'm listening to Pandora. Mark Knopfler is singing in the background. But the moment I pause, the music shifts—first to Leonard Cohen, and then quickly to Zucchero.

I love all three of these artists. Then Pandora cues up Chris Rea, Sting, Sade, Seal, Eros Ramazotti, Depeche Mode, Adele, and Jennifer Hudson. All of this music brings me joy—but each artist finds a different way to touch my soul.

As I listen, I embrace the momentum of the progression, the originality, and the difference in each song. And I find a message in the music that relates exactly to writing about change.

Just as we can love and embrace and draw many emotions from musicians across many styles, so we can embrace change, even find joy in the surprise.

If we could only stay in one place, one snapshot of time—if we could forget change and push away everything new and strange, all the events pressing on us, how would we ever grow?

Isn't life a dance? Isn't life a constant choice? Isn't life made of changes?

In my life, some changes made me grow, contributed to deeper understanding, and helped me learn to love life. I feel lucky that I welcomed those changes.

Everyone's Journey Continues

As I write this, my son and my grandchildren are vacationing in the Bahamas. No doubt, they're experiencing changes that feel magical. They'll have the memories for the rest of their lives, and they can savor those memories—but they can never fully relive those exact moments. Yet, because they took this trip, positive changes will reverberate as long as they live.

The journey always continues. So where am I on my own journey? You already know how much I love the music, the book, the heart ticking—and my passion to share it all with you. I accomplished so many of my dreams—and I'm in a great place.

Yet, I believe there is so much more ahead. In the coming years, I'm expecting even greater happiness and tasty fruits. I taste my sweets and I feel good. But a voice inside me calls me back to the seed that was once so curious and searching.

Am I still curious? What am I looking for?

Yes, I am! I'm still looking for more guidance, and that will continue as long as I live. I feel my partnership with the world around me and the blessings in my life—so what is it that I search for?

I may not know it until I find it. But I know and feel that I am actually looking forward to whatever change is in store for me.

With change newness steps in and pushes aside all the familiarity. It brings us back to that fresh vulnerability and youth.

Interestingly, since I've been writing this book, the nightmare I shared with you earlier has not reappeared. I don't think that's a coincidence. By writing another book, I've opened myself up to change. And maybe, with that new awareness, my subconscious no longer needs to get "lost" before it can be found.

I want to feel and experience new things, acknowledge and welcome new changes. With examples like Grandma Moses, Pablo Casals, and many others who were creative into their 90s, I know that it's still not too late in life to start over. I could learn to paint or play drums...I will definitely explore new places...I could learn other languages (I speak four already) and meet people I've never seen before. I want to talk to them. I want to share my most recent discoveries and all that I have to offer.

Change! So huge and so powerful in our lives!

Once, I even created a game titled "The Change $ Game"

This game is all about providing support, realistic tools and life experience for the players while they find ways to acquire Change Dollars to stay in the game.

Change Dollars—money—is a commodity we must cherish—but only as our servant, never as our master. It can change and influence our lives.

If you ask me at this very moment what I would like to have more than anything, it would be LIBERTY in all facets of life, emotionally, mentally, physically, and financially. I am not so familiar with living in liberty, but it's a change I would embrace. I want to feel free to go places without a worry on my mind, for as long as I wish. Instead of getting lost in my nightmare, I would always find my anchor and my boundaries—so I can be complete and balanced.

What changes are you going through? Are you at

times fearing change? Embracing it? How can I be of help to you?

The answers will light up your personal painting and changes will fill in the colors.

(Bonus) Chapter 11
Intuition

Intuition plays a powerful role in our lives. When we tap into that deep intuition we learn to filter our choices and pursue what feels good and just.

How many times in your life were you feeling overwhelmed or lost—searching for answers in one area or another? And somehow, just then, out of all that chaos, your intuition spoke up with an inner voice that only you could hear?

And you chose.

Often, friends ask what my intuition is telling me about their situation. I sit with the question and let it marinate as I prepare to connect with my intuition.

Once I receive guidance, I suggest the answer. Most of the time, its right on the money. And the choice was healthy, productive, and kind.

Your intuition is a gift you were born with. The DOXA Method will wake up and empower you to tap into it.

Once you've learned to activate it and listen to it, your intuition will filter your choices, show you the correct action, and help you reach your optimal level.

When you use the DOXA Method to rotate through each of the three time zones, your intuition will become stronger and more independent.

Using this process, you will release fear—transforming it into ease as you make the shift to success and happiness.

It's quite interesting how and why intuition works. You may discover that the process works more easily in some areas than in others. For emotional decisions, I find that the rotation becomes slower and slower, just as our metabolism it slows down dramatically as we get older.

What do we do to reduce these effects of aging? We increase our exercise and reduce our food intake, of course. Similarly, to keep our intuition in shape, we reduce the fear by honoring it and transforming it, and harnessing the DOXA Method to work across the three time zones.

What you're really doing is activating the power of attraction. Using DOXA's four steps, you 1) *attract* what you desire, 2) in an *outstanding* fashion, 3) *x out* the debris along your journey, and 4) at all times *allow yourself to be you* and no one else; a total original in shape and form.

This is life—and this is where you learn to transform illusion into reality.

It may surprise you that illusion can be influential and invaluable. In your current reality, you probably experience fear. But as you create the illusion that leads you to a happy and successful place, you will shift the fear to a calmer level—and you, too, will accomplish your dreams one by one. Eventually, the illusion of happiness becomes your new, happy reality.

SECTION 3
THE DOXA METHOD life
with the DOXA METHOD

THE DOXA METHOD QUESTIONS relating to the 3 major benefits:

1. Build a dialogue with your mind!
    - Ask your mind questions
    - Your choices are the responses to these questions
    - With the D0XA Method you filter and marinate the choices
    - You become free and your DESIRE for life is ignited-The first step in the DOXA METHOD

Sample questions:
- How can I let go of the extra weight I carry?
- Why have I chosen my career?
- Am I happy with this union?
- How can I get my children to connect with me?
- Where can I make some changes in my life now?
- Why am I in such a lousy mood?
- Where should we go on vacation this year?
- How can I generate more income?

2. Live and rotate the 3 time zones—skillfully and flowingly—time stops for no one

   The clock design on the back cover of this book reflects the 3 time zones

   The large circle is colored red- this "alarm" color warns us how important it is to learn and practice "letting go"—let go of past emotional challenges and reduce the extra weight we carry to help us enable us to take the driver's seat in our life vehicle

   The red color tells us to **TAKE ACTION**—the past is gone—you need to let it go too

   Extract the seeds of wisdom from the past challenges and experiences

   Bring them into the now—The yellow circle

LIFE WITH THE DOXA METHOD

Focus on the now—act and produce in the now—appreciate the now

The now—the present—empowers us to move forward with our desires and shift from average to OUTSTANDING – the 2nd step in The DOXA Method

Furthermore the actions and the choices we make in the now—lead us to the 3rd step in The DOXA Method. We become so enthused, our desire so elevated, that we produce outstanding results we x-out the impossible and thrive to raise and open doors to all that is possible and achievable

This circle is the middle circle connecting and bridging the past with the future ("post-time")

The smallest area, the heart of the entire circle, is colored in green.

Green stands for optimism, opportunities and having something wonderful to look forward to—worthwhile and with a huge purpose.

This circle is the center and the movement in the rotation. The future—post-time circle—represents the outcome of the 4th step in The DOXA Method success formula (allow you to be you)

Judgment, blame, punishment, anger, and envy are no longer practiced—and so we progress to the 3rd benefit in The DOXA Method: "Transport fears into success"

By allowing us the freedom to honor who and how we are, we automatically become more liberated and more open-minded. We reduce our fears. We eliminate the anxiety we feel day by day. We flow with life.

We can return to building a dialogue with our minds:

We are no longer stressed and feeling intimidated by asking questions.

We grow, we blossom, and we inhale and exhale the beauty of life with all its glory, love and splendor.

The DOXA Method!

Chapter Finale

What's the finale to this book? And what benefits and takeaways will you use for the rest of your life?

My intentions are genuine and authentic. I simply want to be an instrument in transporting your fears, apprehensions, and doubts into success—and help you create a happy environment for you at work, at home, and in between.

You get to a certain place in life where you want to cherish your peace of mind, enjoy your family, retain tremendous joy from your career, and follow a passion that's bigger than your daily routine.

Is it all possible? And is it also workable? Yes! It's all up to us. Remember, we can choose.

Everyone in my office looks forward to the weekend. The weekend represents time off from the work duties, work accomplishments, work expectations, and work responsibilities. Indeed, the weekend stands for more time: to do the things we really love to do, be with the people we want to be with, and perhaps sleep in a few extra hours.

Now let's look at the other side of the coin. On weekends, we also catch up with shopping, cleaning, cooking, and organizing. We meet up with family members/friends, or have guests over.

We don't consider these chores work. Even if they cause some stress, nevertheless, we follow our desires and commit to the choice.

It's all good and this is what life is made of. However we can also choose to appreciate our position in the organization. We can acknowledge that we are co-dependent on others to not just survive but thrive. We can be grateful that we use our minds to think, to solve problems. And we can build for that very special next adventure.

For me, the passion—and the next adventure—usually involves travel. The luggage in the garage is staring at us. When are we going to pack? How much are we packing? What clothes do we need? How can we lighten the load—what can we do without? Perhaps less is more. But let's not forget comfortable walking shoes so we can explore the place.

And every time I think of traveling and going somewhere away from my zip code I remember that story my stepfather Itzhak shared with us 50 years ago—and that I shared with you in Chapter 6.

Itzhak lived a simple life but his mind was rich with common sense and practical ideas. He passed away years ago, but I still cherish his presence, his generosity, and his wisdom.

Every time my feelings and emotions take over and I'm tempted to toss logic and common sense to the other side of the fence. I remember him.

It's all about finding the balance, isn't it?

I hope that THE DOXA Method—empowering you to transport fear into success—gave you not only some productive tools to get to where you want to be on every step of your life journey, but also opened a door for you to find not just happiness, but joy.

And with that, I want to thank you for reading this

book. I hadn't really planned to write it. Yes, somehow, the birth of my past came alive in my current reality and mixed with my colorful illusions and dreams—and I had to share it with you.

If you take one thing away from reading this book, let it be this: You don't need to live with regrets. If you live a life you feel good about, then even if the choices you made in the past weren't the ones you'd make today, they still turned out okay.

Of course, you may wonder at times, "if only..." And if you're not happy in your current life, it's never too late to make things better. Always remember that your real job is to make the best reality for yourself that you can at this moment—and let that magical reality spread to the larger world.

With a huge smile on my face and deep gratitude that you came with me on this journey, I am here for you. Reach me at ana@anaweberdoxa.com

I embrace life, and I love life with you in it!

Ana Weber

About Ana Weber...Business "Rainmaker," Writer, Speaker, 360 Degree Lifestyle Leadership Coach-Relationship Expert, Founder of the DOXA METHOD, and Philanthropist

The consummate "people person," Ana approaches every person and every new experience with joy and love. Her employees love to work with her, and her friends love to be around her. And at every company she has helped to manage, she's helped engineer massive revenue growth. As an example, she took one company from annual revenues of $250,000 to $82 million in just five years, while creating 83 new full-time jobs. If you ask Ana the secret of her long string of business successes, she'll tell you it's all about building relationships.

In addition to her many decades of business experience, Ana has achieved success in multiple parallel careers— as a writer, speaker, personal and business/professional coach, and philanthropist:

Writer:

Since 2005, she's published 19 nonfiction books on personal improvement, covering personal happiness, time management, healthy eating, business/personal success, parenting and money relationships, leadership as well as a novel and a poetry collection. Her books have been featured on some of the top websites in the world, including SheKnows.com, VenusDivas.com, and Divorce. com., American Airlines, USA Weekly, Wall Street Journal and Bank of America Newsletter April 2014.

As a freelance journalist who has published in Parents Magazine, Lifestyle, USA Today, USA Weekly, Wall Street Journal, Bank of America, American Airlines on flight Magazine, Celebrity, Orange County Register, and TV Guide, she has interviewed dozens of high-profile high achievers, among them supermodel Kathy Ireland, anti-aging expert Dr. William Andrews, and Melanie True Hills—e-business strategist, author, and founder and CEO of the American Foundation for Women's Health. (Detailed list of interviewees and publications on request.)

Speaker:

Ana's recent presentations include Canyon Ranch, Avalon European River Cruises (general public); Southwest Airlines, ADP, JetBlue, Virgin Atlantic (corporate), American Institute of Architects National Conference, University of Michigan Annual Education Conference, Eastern Michigan University (academic and professional organizations). University of Delaware, Cal Poly, San Luis Obispo, Author 101 University and High Point University, Harvard Business School, West Point Military Academy, New York University, ECA 360- Fitness, N.Y., University of Arizona, Tucson. Universal Music Headquarters, London. TM Forum Digital Communications Conference, Nice, France.

Founder of the 360 Degrees of Success course on <u>www. udemy.com</u> and founder of the DOXA METHOD, www.

*anawberdoxa.com*Ana provides individuals and groups with practical tools to maintain a high energy level... merge their passion, talents, skills, educations and experiences...live in the present...and, most importantly, live a balanced, joyful, and successful life linking the 4 essential ingredients money-relationships-energy-time. Ana empowers individuals and organizations to reach their optimal level of achievements-influential leadership-focus – letting go and flow with change, live in the three time zones.

Philanthropist:

Known for her generosity in the charity and celebrity world, Ana raises funds for the American Heart Association, American Cancer Society, Children's Hospitals; Los Angeles, Atlanta and Heifer International. She has participated and given away gift packaging containing her products at various events including the American Music Awards, Golden Globe Awards, Google Awards, Academy Awards and Hoodie Awards., Women of Global Change, Institute for Humane Education and College Summit.

Books by Ana Weber:

o   Companion workbook to Passion Spirit Purpose

o   Passion Spirit Purpose

o   360 Degrees of Success!

o   The money flow, have a great life and improve the world

o   Sweet Nothings - Lead you to everything, an inspirational journal (English –Spanish version)

o   The Circle of Success - is waiting for you; book/ program

o   Eat the foods that love you back - 3 simple steps to love what you eat!!!

o   I love Monday's

o   We are not islands

o   The Happiness Thermometer

o   ETM the Circle of Success

o   Your 48 hour day

o   Apples. Eggs, onions A diet for Change

o   A diet for change

o   Dumped – The Ultimate guide to starting over

o   Lemons into Lemonade without the sugar

o   11 step formula to bridge the gap between parents and teenagers

o   Silky Emotions (poetry)

Education: Masters of Business Administration, Ashworth University

Continued education Oxford University, Brookes College Ph.D, Philosophy

BA International Business-University of Tel Aviv

Additional certification with IPEC – CPC and Master Practitioner Coach

National Speakers Association Professional Member

Media

Ana Weber

Has been interviewed extensively on television including:

- ❖ FOX NEWS
- ❖ ABC San Francisco
- ❖ Good Day New York
- ❖ NBC Chicago
- ❖ NBC South Florida
- ❖ ABC Phoenix
- ❖ UNIVISION
- ❖ Bloomberg-Spotlight TV
- ❖ CBS Denver
- ❖ KUSI 9 San Diego
- ❖ Celebrity TV
- ❖ Fox Houston
- ❖ NBC Austin
- ❖ FOX L.A.
- ❖ NBC St. Louis
- ❖ Moving America Forward – with William Shatner

Articles by and about Ana have appeared in print media including:

- ❖ USA TODAY
- ❖ Wall Street Journal
- ❖ Woman's World
- ❖ COSMOPOLITAN
- ❖ Chicago Sun Star
- ❖ Fairfax Times
- ❖ O.C. Metro
- ❖ Copley News
- ❖ Thrillist
- ❖ Erie Magazine
- ❖ Philadelphia Edge
- ❖ Herald May
- ❖ O.C Register
- ❖ L.A. Times
- ❖ Chicago Tribune
- ❖ Atlanta Journal Constitution
- ❖ Daily Camera
- ❖ Celebrity News
- ❖ Huffington Post
- ❖ Prevention

Ana has appeared on syndicated nationwide radio shows including:

- ❖ Be the Star You Are
- ❖ Straight Line Talk
- ❖ ABC Radio
- ❖ XM Radio
- ❖ The Bev Smith Show
- ❖ The Nigro Show
- ❖ ABC radio Live

- ❖ WMET Washington
- ❖ The New Lifestyle Radio
- ❖ Internet Radio
- ❖ Playboy Radio
- ❖ Table Talk Santa Barbara
- ❖ Clear Channel Radio, Philadelphia
- ❖ Frankie Boyer show